1.50

QUEST 2000
EXPLORING MATHEMATICS

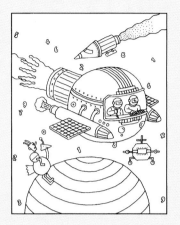

Math·a·pedia

AUTHORS

Randall I. Charles   Brendan Kelly   David C. Brummett
Ricki Wortzman   Lalie Harcourt   Carne S. Barnett

CONTRIBUTING AUTHORS

Elisabeth Javor
Alma Ramirez
Freddie Lee Renfro
Mary M. Soniat-Thompson

Addison-Wesley Publishing Company
Menlo Park, California; Reading,
Massachusetts; New York;
Don Mills, Ontario; Wokingham,
England; Amsterdam; Bonn;
Paris; Milan; Madrid; Sydney;
Singapore; Tokyo; Seoul; Taipei;
Mexico City; San Juan

INTERMEDIATE

Design: MKR Design, Inc.

Cover Design: The Pushpin Group

The TI-12 Explorer is a trademark of Texas Instruments Incorporated.
The map on page 20 is from *Student's Atlas of the World*, page 11.
Copyright © 1987 by American Map Corporation.

ISBN 0-201-84121-5

2 3 4 5 6 7 8 9 10 VH 98 97 96 95

TABLE of Contents

Words AND *Ideas*

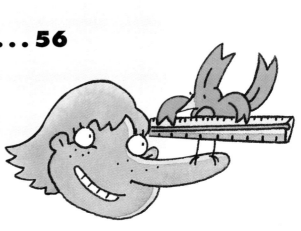

Formulas and Equivalencies

Technology

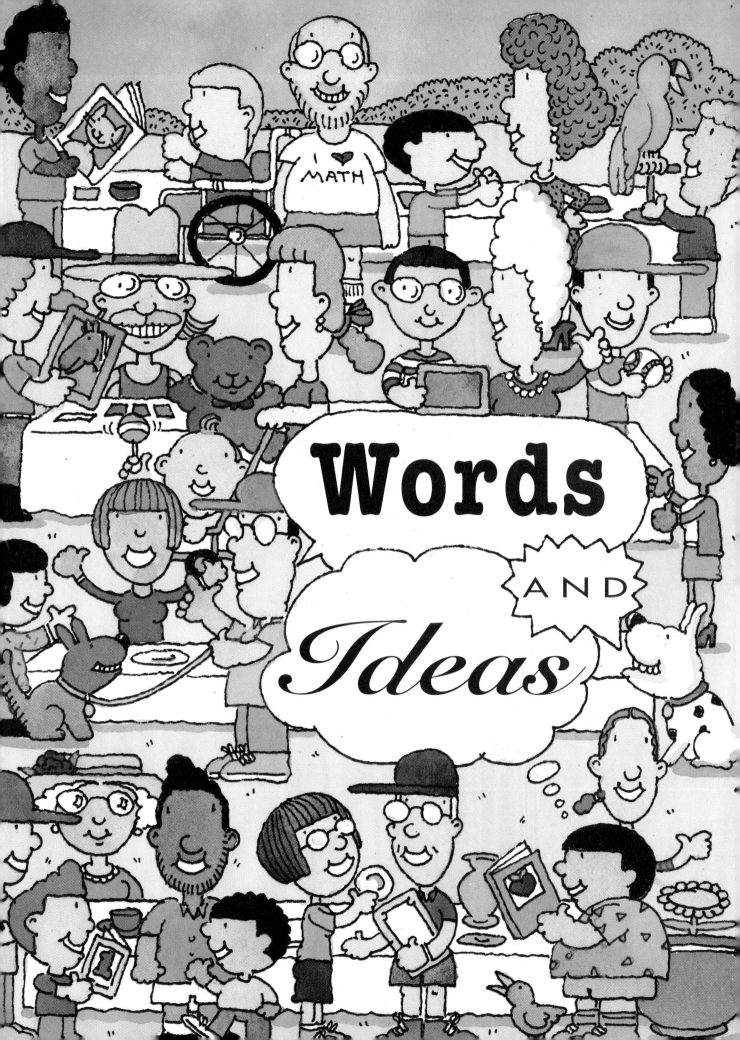

Addition

Addition is an operation that gives the total when you **combine** two or more groups.

Sometimes you can actually combine the two groups to find the total.

Sometimes you have to imagine the groups being combined.

There are fourteen trees in all.

There are certain names and symbols we use when we record addition.

$$23 + 13 = 36$$

| addend | addition symbol | addend | equal symbol | sum |

There are many ways to do addition.

$$46 + 38 =$$

$$40 + 30 = 70$$
$$6 + 8 = 14$$

$$\begin{array}{r} 70 \\ +14 \\ \hline 84 \end{array}$$

First I'll add the tens.

Then I'll add the ones.

I'll add the ones first.

Then I'll add the tens.

$$\begin{array}{r} 1 \\ 46 \\ +38 \\ \hline 84 \end{array}$$

I can add these in my head.

38 is about 40.

46 plus 40 is 86.

I added 2 too many so I have to take 2 away.

86 minus 2 is 84.

The sum is 84.

I think I'll use a calculator.

I'll estimate first.

46 is about 50 and 38 is about 40.

I know that 50 plus 40 equals 90 so the answer is close to 90.

Addition and subtraction are related.

Because **34 + 18 = 52** then **52 − 18 = 34** and **52 − 34 = 18**.

Addition is also related to multiplication. Multiplication is repeated addition.

5 + 5 + 5 + 5 can be written **4 x 5**.

Find out more about *subtraction* on pages 100–103.
Find out more about *multiplication* on pages 63–67.

Angle

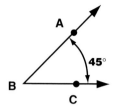

An **angle** is formed by two **rays** with the same endpoint. The endpoint is called a **vertex**.

The size or amount of opening of an angle is measured using a unit called a **degree**. The symbol for degrees is °.

Angle *ABC* has a measure of **45°**.

These two rays meet at vertex *B* to form angle *ABC*.

We write: ∠*ABC*

An **angle bisector** is a ray that divides an angle into two angles of equal measure.

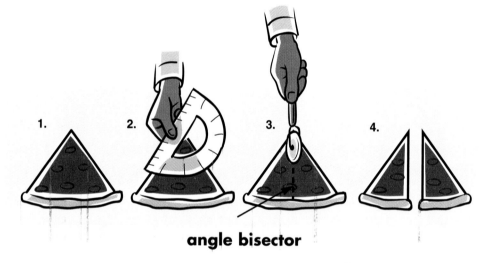

1.   2.   3.   4.

angle bisector

We have names for some angles.

The angle between the big hand and the small hand has a measure of **90°**. Such an angle is called a **right angle**.

Now the angle between the big hand and the small hand has a measure **less than 90°**. Such an angle is called an **acute angle**.

Look at the clock, now. The angle between the big hand and the small hand is an **obtuse angle**. This means that the angle measures **more than 90°** but **less than 180°**.

We can measure angles using a **protractor**.

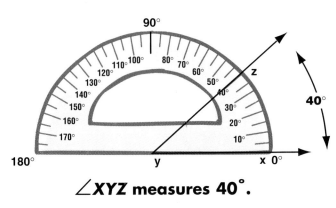

∠XYZ measures 40°.

To measure an angle using a protractor, first place the center point of the protractor on the vertex of the angle. Then make sure that the zero edge of the protractor is along one ray of the angle. Now see what number the other ray is indicating. This is the measure of the angle.

We can also use an **angle ruler** to measure and draw angles.

To draw an angle measuring **105°**, hold down the side of the angle ruler that has the angle markings on it. Then rotate the other side of the angle ruler until it is lined up with 105°. Now use the edges of the ruler to draw the angle.

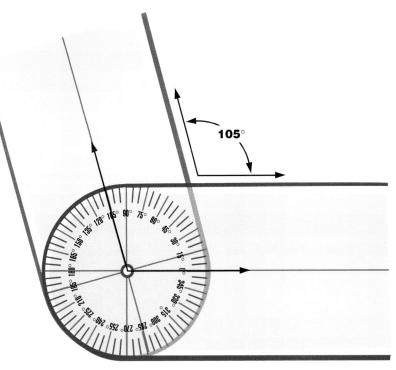

Area

Area is the amount of space a figure or shape occupies. We measure area in square units.

All of these rectangles have the same area even though their dimensions are different.

1 x 12 = 12 square units

2 x 6 = 12 square units

3 x 4 = 12
square units

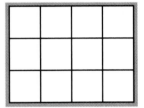

I need to cover all four sides as well as the top and bottom of this box.

Surface area is the sum of the areas of all the faces of a three-dimensional figure.

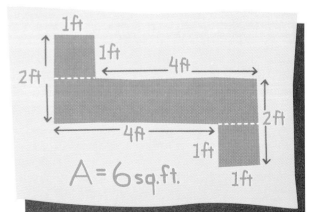

Sometimes we must find the area of an irregular shape. In this case, we often can find the area by adding or subtracting the areas of the smaller shapes that make up the irregular shape.

1ft
1ft
4ft
2ft
4ft
2ft
1ft
1ft

A = 6 sq.ft.

Find out more about *area formulas* on pages 116–120.

An **array** is an arrangement of objects in rows and columns. Arrays give us a special way to look at equal groups.

column column column

row

row

row

row

row

6 x 4 = 24 cans

When I see the word **array**, I think of the word **arrangement**, because they start with the same letters.

5 x 3 = 15 boxes

Average

In daily conversation, we often use the word **average**.

In these cases the word **average** means typical, common, or ordinary.

She is an average height for a nine year old.

Today was an average day at school.

I read an average of about one chapter a day.

He's not a great player, just an average one!

In mathematics an average is a quantity that summarizes a set of data. Averages can be used to determine what is typical or common.

The average length of a newborn is **20** inches.

The average high temperature for this date is **75** degrees.

The mean is the most commonly used average. To find an average of a set of data you can:

Add all the numbers in the set. Then divide that sum by the number of items in the set.

The average allowance in this family of three children is;

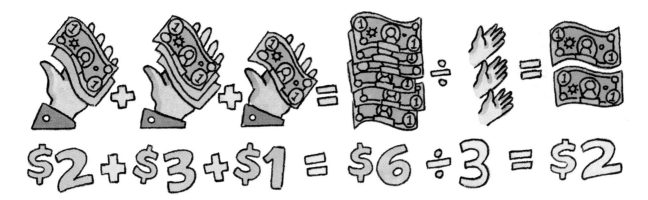

$$\$2 + \$3 + \$1 = \$6 \div 3 = \$2$$

I'm designing a new clothing line for teens. I need to know the average sleeve length.

There are many situations where you might want to calculate an average.

I want to know the batting average of my favorite baseball player.

Find out more about *mean* on page 55 and *statistics* on pages 98–99.

Capacity

Capacity (liquid measure) is the amount of liquid a container can hold.

We can measure liquid using customary and metric units:

fluid ounces (fl oz)   **cups (c)**   **pints (pt)**   **quarts (qt)**   **gallons (gal)**   **milliliters (mL)**   **liters (L)**

We often need to measure liquids when we use a recipe.

We need half a gallon of milk and two bananas.

I'll add the two teaspoons of vanilla to the pint of yogurt while you get the milk and bananas.

Find out more about *capacity* on page 121.

Chance is the likelihood that a particular event will occur.

Words like *chance* are used to anticipate future events such as weather and raffle outcomes.

It looks like a fifty percent chance of rain sometime on the weekend.

Why did you buy a raffle ticket? Your chances of winning the big prize are less than one in eight hundred.

Students sometimes talk about chances.

Mom, my chances of doing well are not good. I'll be lucky to pass my science test.

Well, someone has to win, and my chances are as good as anyone's.

I discovered that the harder I studied—the luckier I got.

Sometimes I wish my mother wasn't a professor of statistics.

Find out more about *statistics* on pages 98–99.

A **circle** is a set of points that are all the same distance from a point called the **center**.

The diagram below shows several **circles** and their **centers**.

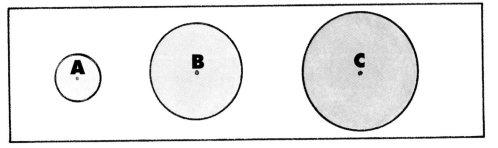

The smallest circle has its center at point *A*. All the points on the small circle are the same distance from *A*. Also all the points on the large circle are the same distance from its center, *C*.

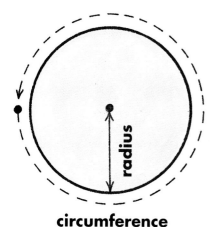

circumference

The distance around a circle is called the **circumference**. The distance from the center to any point on the circle is called the **radius**.

A line from one point on the circle to another point on the circle that passes through the center is called the **diameter**. The diameter cuts the circle in half. The length of the diameter of a circle is double the length of the radius of the circle.

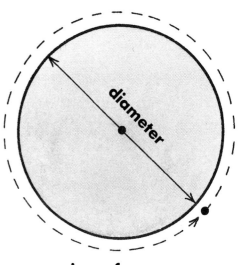

circumference

If we divide the circumference of any circle by its diameter, we get a number which is approximately **3.14**.

We write:

$$\frac{\text{circumference}}{\text{diameter}} \quad \textbf{is approximately equal to } 3.14.$$

The exact value of this fraction is a non-repeating decimal. We represent it by the Greek letter π, which is pronounced like the word *pie* but is spelled **pi**. A good fractional estimate of π is $\frac{22}{7}$.

For thousands of years, humans have tried to find a fraction to approximate π. The table below shows some of these fractions.

CIVILIZATION	DATE	FRACTION USED TO APPROXIMATE π
Babylonians	1700 BC	$3\frac{1}{8}$
Greeks	220 BC	$3\frac{1}{7}$
Chinese	470 AD	$\frac{355}{113}$
Hindus	1150 AD	$\frac{3927}{1250}$

The first few digits of π are **3.14159**. You can use your calculator to find out which of the civilizations in the table above had the best approximation to π.

Let's see, that's about 3.14 times 5 times 5—which is 78.5 square inches.

We need to find the area of our nest. The radius of the nest is 5 inches.

See, even round things have areas in square inches.

Find out more about *circles* in Formulas and Equivalencies on pages 116–119.

Composite Numbers

A **composite number** has more than two factors.

Numbers such as **6**, **20**, and **26** are composite numbers.

Composite numbers can be displayed as arrays with more than one row.

All even numbers except the number **2** are composite numbers.

Here are the composite numbers less than 30.
4, 6, 8, 9, 10, 12, 14, 15, 16, 18, 20, 21, 22, 24, 25, 26, 27, 28

Find out more about *composite numbers* on page 83.

Congruent Figures

Two geometric figures are **congruent** when they are the same shape and same size. Congruent figures are identical, and they cover each other exactly. These are examples of some things that suggest the idea of congruence.

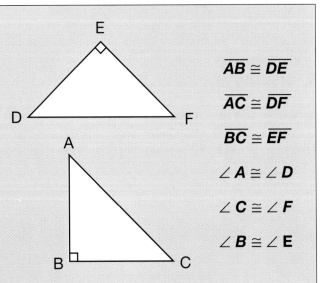

The symbol ≅ means *is congruent to*.

△ **ABC** ≅ △ **DEF**. We say that triangle **ABC** is congruent to triangle **DEF**. This means that the two triangles have matching congruent angles and matching congruent sides. △ **ABC** fits exactly on △ **DEF**.

$\overline{AB} \cong \overline{DE}$

$\overline{AC} \cong \overline{DF}$

$\overline{BC} \cong \overline{EF}$

∠ **A** ≅ ∠ **D**

∠ **C** ≅ ∠ **F**

∠ **B** ≅ ∠ **E**

congruent figures

The shape and size of the figures do not change if the direction is changed. The figures are still congruent to one another.

We can slide, turn, and flip shapes to see if they are congruent.

1. Here is how we can check congruency.

2. Trace one shape.

3. Turn the tracing to see if it matches the other shape.

4. If the shapes match they are congruent figures.

Coordinate System

A **coordinate system** is a way to tell location. It is made up of vertical and horizontal number lines. The horizontal line is called the **x-axis**. The vertical line is called the **y-axis**. The **origin** is the point where these lines meet.

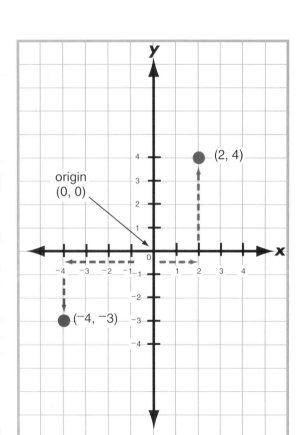

We use **coordinates** or **ordered pairs** to describe a point. The first coordinate tells the distance right or left on the x-axis. The second coordinate tells the distance up or down on the y-axis.

When we mark a point for the coordinates, we are **graphing** or **plotting** a point.

Data

Data is information. Data can be collected from sources such as books, newspapers, and television.

Mount Everest is 29,078 feet high.

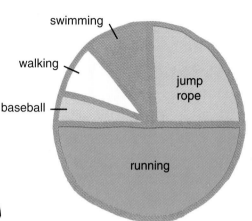

swimming

walking

baseball

jump rope

running

This graph shows the amount of aerobic energy used in exercise.

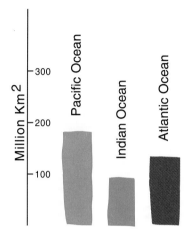

Million Km²

300

200

100

Pacific Ocean

Indian Ocean

Atlantic Ocean

This table shows the areas of each of the world's oceans.

Data can also be obtained through **surveys**. Two common types of surveys are **interviews** and **questionnaires**.

An **experiment** is another means of obtaining data.

An **interview** is a planned set of questions that is asked orally by the interviewer.

A **questionnaire** is a set of questions that is asked and answered in writing.

what is the relationship between the height from which the ball is dropped and the height to which the ball bounces?

Data Organization

When we have a lot of data, it is useful to display the data in an organized way. An organized display helps us to interpret and answer questions. We use **tables** and **graphs** to display data.

There are many different kinds of **graphs**.

A **picture graph** or **pictograph** is a graph that uses pictures to represent one or more objects in the collection of data. A picture graph should have a **key** that tells what number each picture represents.

Number of CD's sold by the top four bands	
Bands	**CD's sold**
The Zots	◎ ◎ ◎
Noon	◎ ◎
Split Bananas	◎ ◖
Planet Q	◎ ◎ ◎ ◎
	◎ =20,000 ◖ =10,000

Tally marks can be used to keep track of objects when counting. Tally marks are arranged in groups of five, with the fifth mark across the first four.

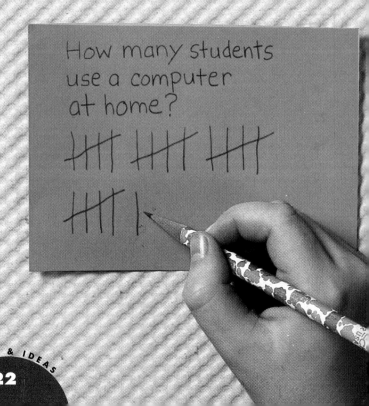

How many students use a computer at home?

卌 卌 卌

卌 I

A **bar graph** uses horizontal or vertical bars of equal width but different heights (or lengths) to show information. Bar graphs are used to compare data. The horizontal and vertical numbers are sometimes called the **horizontal axis** and **vertical axis**.

Monthly Earnings from Bagel Sales

Vertical axis

Grades

Horizontal axis

Amount of money collected

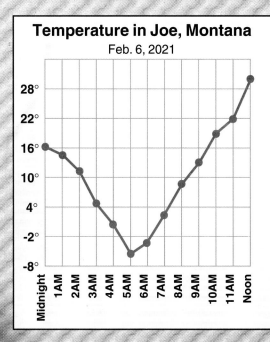

Temperature in Joe, Montana
Feb. 6, 2021

A **line graph** is a diagram that uses a rising or falling line to show patterns or changes in data over a period of time.

The times along the bottom of the graph show the **horizontal scale**. The temperatures along the side of the graph show the **vertical scale**.

The **interval** is the number of units between spaces on a graph's scale.

This graph is called a **line plot** or a **number-line plot**. The horizontal scale shows how many people in a family.

A line plot is a kind of pictograph in which the vertical scale shows the frequency of an event or occurrence. A line plot makes it easy to see which is the greatest number and least number in a collection of data. It also shows us which number occurred most often, or the **mode**.

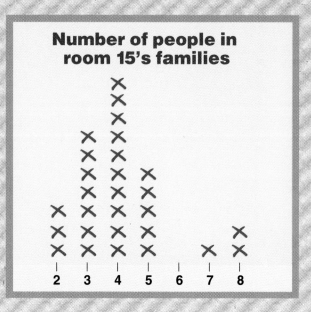

Number of people in room 15's families

A **circle graph**, often called a **pie chart**, is used to show how the whole is broken into parts.

Sometimes it is difficult to understand the relationships among the data. We can use a **Venn diagram** to help us.

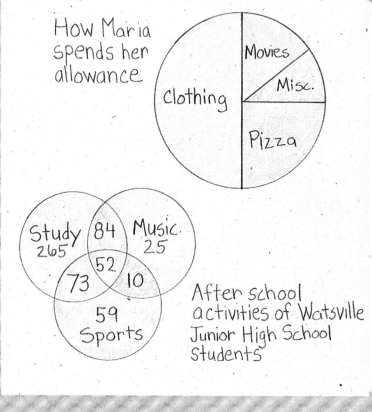

How Maria spends her allowance

Movies
Misc.
Clothing
Pizza

Study 265
84
Music 25
52
73
10
59 Sports

After school activities of Watsville Junior High School Students

Prices of Video Games

2	9.99
3	5, 6.99, 9.90, 9.90, 9.90 9.99
4	2.49, 2.49, 2.49, 2.49, 2.49, 4.90, 4.99, 4.99, 4.99, 4.99, 6.99, 8.00, 9.90, 9.90, 9.97, 9.97, 9.99
5	4, 4.99, 6.99

The display shown to the left is a **stem-and-leaf plot**. This plot groups together all amounts with the same number of tens (called the **stem**). Following the stem, the other digits (called the **leaf**) are listed.

The stem-and-leaf plot enables us to compare the number of video games costing between **$29.99** and **$56.99**.

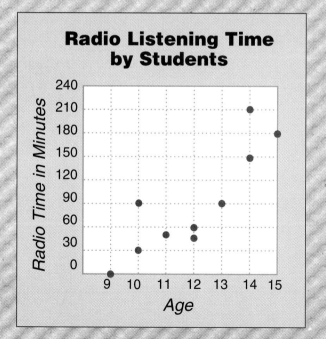

Radio Listening Time by Students

A **scattergram**, sometimes called a **scatterplot**, is a graph of a set of points that compare two sets of data. If the points on a scattergram group together in a certain pattern, then the two sets are probably related.

The scatterplot shows that radio-listening time by students is related to their age. The older the students, the more time they seem to spend listening to the radio.

Find out more about *data* on pages 98–99.

Decimals

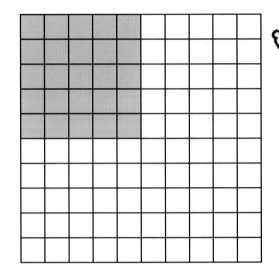

Decimal numbers contain a decimal point. The digits to the right of the decimal point represent a **decimal fraction**, which has as denominator a power of **10,** such as **10, 100**, or **1000**.

$$\frac{1}{4} = \frac{25}{100} = 0.25$$

decimal point   **decimal fraction**

twenty-three and forty-six hundredths

FINISH

23.46

> This swimmer's time will be recorded as 53.872 seconds.

We say "fifty-three and eight hundred seventy-two thousandths." We say thousandths, because the last digit of the decimal number is in the thousandths place.

A **repeating decimal** is a decimal in which a digit or series of digits repeats endlessly.

In **0.575757...** the three dots indicate an endless number of digits follows. We could also write $0.\overline{57}$. The bar over the 57 indicates that this pair of digits is repeated endlessly. We write $0.\overline{3}$ to mean **0.3333...**.

A **terminating decimal** is a decimal that can be written with an exact number of digits such as **0.315** or **0.75234**.

We can find a **decimal equivalent** for a fraction by dividing the numerator by the denominator.

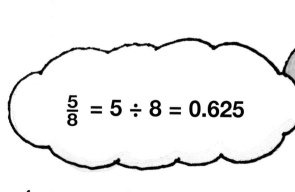

$$\frac{5}{8} = 5 \div 8 = 0.625$$

Find out more about *fractions* on page 37–41.
Find out more about *decimals* and *place value* on page 80.

Division

Division is an operation we use when we want to break a quantity into smaller groups. Say we want a certain number of smaller equal groups, and we need to determine the number in each group. Or say we know how many we want in each group, and we need to determine the number of equal groups. In either situation we use division.

We use special words and symbols to show division.

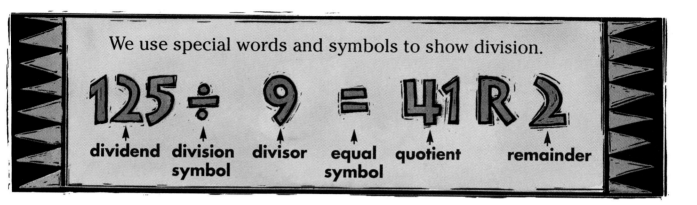

125 ÷ 9 = 41 R 2

dividend · division symbol · divisor · equal symbol · quotient · remainder

There are different ways to divide.

225 ÷ 12

I use multiplication to divide. I need to find how many 12s are in 225.

12 x 10 = 120   so   225 – 120 = 105

12 x 8 = 96   then   105 – 96 = 9

10 + 8 = 18

There are 18 twelves in 225 and 9 left over.

225 ÷ 12 = 18 R 9

I divide in my head
while I record on paper.

$12\overline{)225}$

Where should I write the first digit in the answer?
12 is too big to divide into 2, but it can divide into
22. How many 12s are there in 22?

$12\overline{)22^{1}5}$

There is 1 twelve in 22 and 10 left over.

$12\overline{)22^{10}5}\ \ 18\ R9$

How many 12s are there in 105?
There are eight 12s in 105 with 9
left over. The quotient is 18
remainder 9.

I know another way to divide.

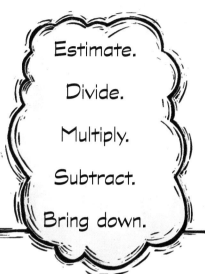

Estimate.

Divide.

Multiply.

Subtract.

Bring down.

$$12\overline{)225.00}$$

```
        1 8. 7 5
12 ) 2 2 5. 0 0
     -1 2 ↓
       1 0 5
     -   9 6 ↓
             9 0
           -8 4 ↓
                 6 0
```

Division is related to subtraction.

84 ÷ 14 is the same as

84 − 14 = 70 − 14 = 56 − 14 =
42 − 14 = 28 − 14 = 14 − 14 = 0

There are 6 groups of 14 in 84. 84 ÷ 14 = 6

Division is related to multiplication.

21 x 35 = 735 so 735 ÷ 21 = 35 and 735 ÷ 35 = 21.

We can use the connection between multiplication and division to check division.

212 ÷ 18 = 11 R 14

Check: 18 x 11 = 198   198 + 14 = 212

Multiply the divisor   **Add the remainder.**
by the quotient.

It's correct!

Equation

An **equation** is a **number sentence** that uses the equal symbol to show that two expressions have the same value.

2 + 5 = 7 is a number sentence or an equation.

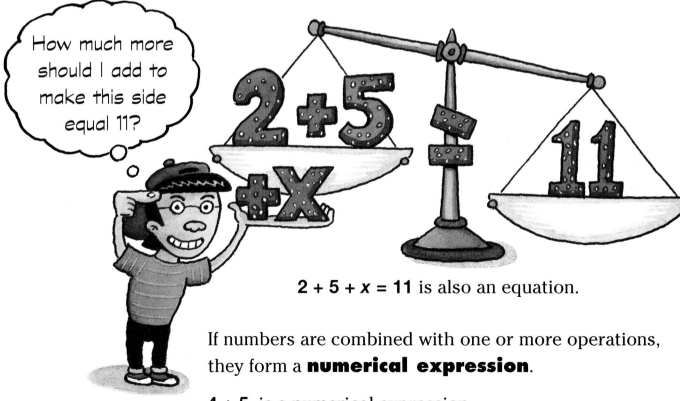

How much more should I add to make this side equal 11?

2 + 5 + *x* = 11 is also an equation.

If numbers are combined with one or more operations, they form a **numerical expression**.

4 + 5 is a numerical expression.

Equations often include a **variable**. A variable is a letter, such as *x*, that stands for a quantity that can change or vary. We use variables in **algebraic expressions**.

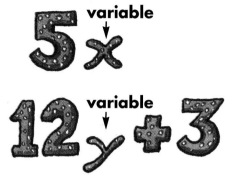

variable
$$5x$$

variable
$$12y + 3$$

A **solution** for an algebraic equation is a value or values for the variable that makes the left side of the equation equal to the right side.

How much does Herman weigh?

$$x + 40 = 100$$

$$60 + 40 = 100$$

So, $x = 60$

The solution is 60 pounds.

A **formula** is an equation that is a general rule expressed by symbols. We can use formulas to help us find the areas of shapes and the volumes of geometric solids.

Find out more about *formulas* on pages 116–120.

Estimate

An **estimate** is a value that is close to the exact answer. We can use **estimation** to check on the reasonableness of an exact answer.

Estimates are used when we cannot determine the exact number or when we only need to know the approximate number.

> $2.00 plus $4.00 plus $3.00 plus $3.00 plus $2.00.

> That's $14.00. With tax, $15.00 seems reasonable.

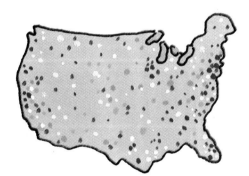

The population of the United States according to the 1990 census was about **248** billion.

A stack of one trillion dollar bills would be about **625** thousand miles high.

Benchmark estimation is using an object of known measurement to estimate the measurement of another object.

> This stick is about 5 inches, so this must be about 25 inches.

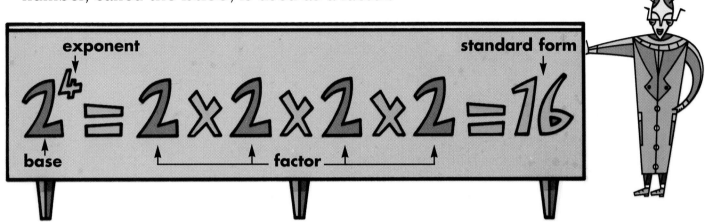

Sometimes we multiply a number by itself several times. The **exponent** tells how many times the number, called the **base**, is used as a factor.

exponent

standard form

$$2^4 = 2 \times 2 \times 2 \times 2 = 16$$

base

factor

We read 2^4 as "two to the fourth **power**" or we can say, "the number two raised to the power of four."

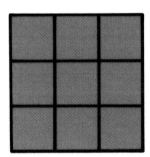

$3 \times 3 = 9$

$3^2 = 9$

We read 3^2 as "three **squared**."

Area = 9 square units

$5 \times 5 \times 5 = 125$

$5^3 = 125$

We read 5^3 as "five **cubed**."

Volume = 125 cubic units

Ten to the sixth power. That means ten times itself six times. $10 \times 10 \times 10 \times 10 \times 10 \times 10 =$ 1 million

Factor

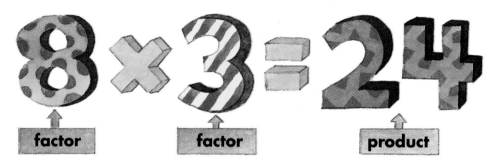

Factors are the numbers that are combined in a multiplication sentence to give another number called a **product**.

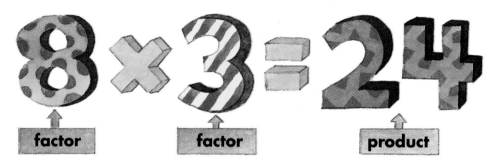

| factor | factor | product |

We can write **24** as a product of two factors in different ways:

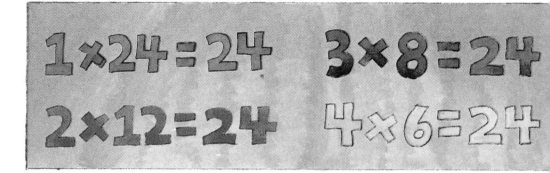

$$1 \times 24 = 24 \qquad 3 \times 8 = 24$$
$$2 \times 12 = 24 \qquad 4 \times 6 = 24$$

The factors of **24** are **1, 2, 3, 4, 6, 8, 12,** and **24**.

The **Greatest Common Factor (GCF)** is the greatest number that is a factor of each of two or more numbers.

In this diagram, the common factors of **18** and **24** are in the region where the circles overlap.

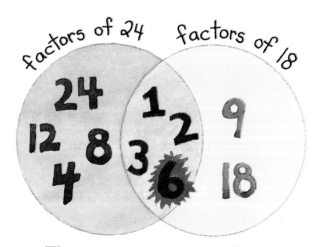

The greatest common factor of **18** and **24** is **6**.

Find out more about *factors* on pages 63–67 and page 83.

A **fraction** is a comparison of a part to a whole.

When we divide a whole or a group into **equal parts**, each part is the same size.

Three fourths of the pizza is left.

$\frac{3}{4}$ $\frac{\text{parts of pizza left}}{\text{equal parts in all}}$

Three fourths of the pizzas are pepperoni.

$\frac{3}{4}$ $\frac{\text{pepperoni pizzas}}{\text{pizzas in all}}$

$\frac{3}{4}$ $\frac{\text{numerator}}{\text{denominator}}$ $\frac{\text{number of equal parts considered}}{\text{equal parts in all}}$

We use special words to talk about fractions with the same denominator.

halves	**thirds**	**fourths or quarters**	**fifths**

 $\frac{1}{2}$ $\frac{1}{3}$ $\frac{3}{4}$ $\frac{2}{5}$

 $\frac{3}{2}$ $\frac{2}{3}$  $\frac{4}{4}$ $\frac{6}{5}$

A **proper fraction** has a numerator that is less than the denominator. Proper fractions with number **1** as a numerator are called **unit fractions**.

$$\frac{2}{5} \quad \frac{3}{4} \quad \frac{5}{8} \qquad \frac{1}{10} \quad \frac{1}{2}$$

unit fractions

An **improper fraction** has a numerator that is greater than or equal to the denominator.

$$\frac{3}{2} \quad \frac{4}{3} \quad \frac{9}{9} \quad \frac{7}{4} \quad \frac{11}{8}$$

Mixed numbers and **improper fractions** name parts of wholes greater than or equal to **1**.

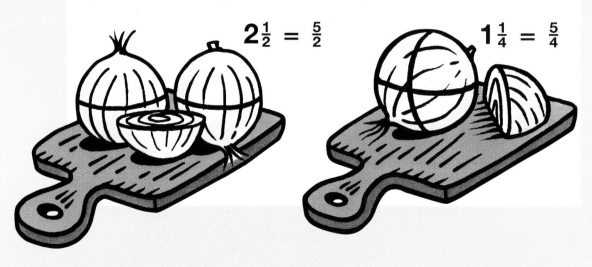

$$2\frac{1}{2} = \frac{5}{2} \qquad\qquad 1\frac{1}{4} = \frac{5}{4}$$

We can use a chart like this one to compare fractions.

$$\frac{2}{4} < \frac{2}{3}$$

Two fourths is less than two thirds.

$$\frac{3}{4} > \frac{3}{8}$$

Three fourths is greater than three eighths.

Different fractions that name the same amount are called **equivalent fractions**.

$\frac{3}{4}$ is equivalent to $\frac{6}{8}$.

To make an equivalent fraction, you can multiply the numerator and the denominator of a fraction by any number but zero.

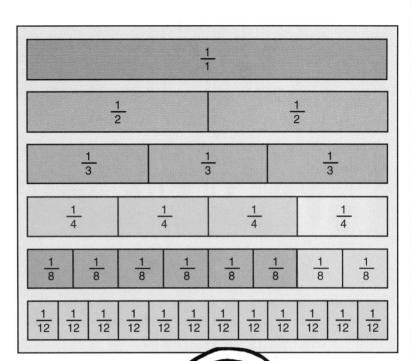

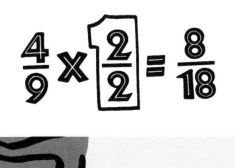

$$\frac{4}{9} \times \frac{2}{2} = \frac{8}{18}$$

Fractions that have the same denominator are said to have **common denominators**. Fractions with common denominators are called **like fractions**.

Sometimes we **rename fractions** so they have the same denominator.

 $\frac{1}{4} = \frac{2}{8}$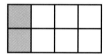

A fraction is in **lowest terms** or **simplest form** when the greatest common factor of the numerator and the denominator is **1**.

$\frac{5}{8}$ is in lowest terms. Only the number **1** will divide evenly into both **5** and **8**.

$\frac{6}{8}$ is not in lowest terms. The greatest common factor of **6** and **8** is **2**.

Fractions and **decimals** are related.

We can **change a fraction to a decimal** by writing an equivalent fraction with a denominator of **10**, **100**, **1,000**, **10,000**, and so on.

$\frac{3}{10} = 0.3$

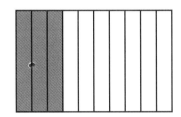

$\frac{47}{100} = 0.47$

When we want to change $\frac{1}{25}$ to a decimal, we can rename the fraction so it has a denominator of **100**.

$\frac{1}{25} = \frac{?}{100}$ $\frac{1}{25} = \frac{1 \times 4}{25 \times 4} = \frac{4}{100} = 0.04$

Another way to change a fraction to a decimal is to divide the numerator by the denominator.

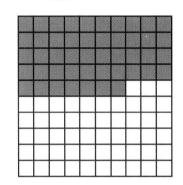

$\frac{1}{10} = 10\overline{)1.0}\ \ ^{0.1}$

$\frac{3}{4} = 4\overline{)3.00}\ \ ^{0.75}$

Find out more about *decimals* on pages 26–27.

Geometric Figures

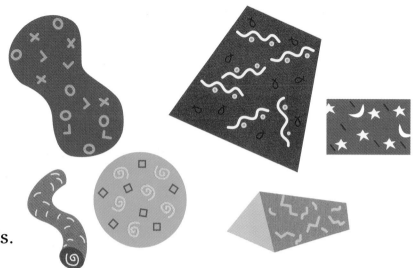

A **geometric figure** is any arrangement of points, lines, curves, or planes. A **plane figure** is a geometric figure drawn on a flat surface.

Geometric figures include curves drawn on a surface, surfaces themselves, and solids.

A **closed figure** is a plane figure that encloses an area.

These are closed plane figures.

These are not closed plane figures.

Geometric figures can be either **regular** or **irregular**.

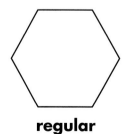 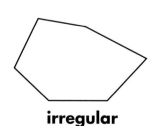

regular   irregular

Find out more about *geometric figures* on pages 81–82 and 90.

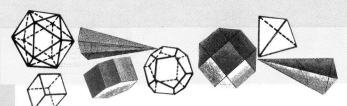

Geometric Solids

Geometric solids or **space figures** are three-dimensional models. Geometric solids have volume. Since the beginning of recorded history, humans have modeled geometric solids in their buildings and structures.

Three solid figures that are related to the circle are **cylinders**, **cones**, and **spheres**.

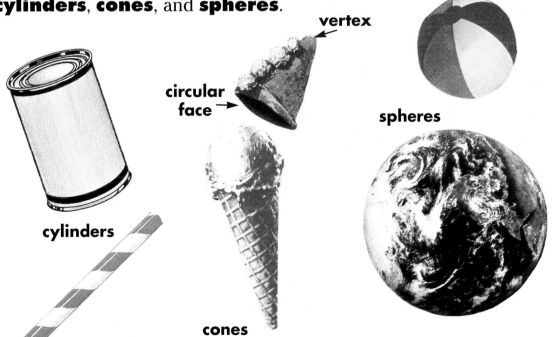

vertex

circular face →

spheres

cylinders

cones

Faces are the flat surfaces of a geometric solid. A pair of faces meet in a line segment called an **edge**. A **vertex** is a point where two or more edges intersect. The **base** is the bottom of a solid.

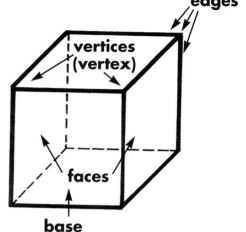

If we expand a polygon vertically we form a **prism**.

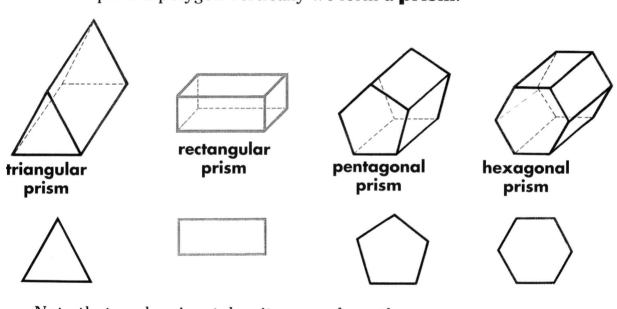

triangular prism   rectangular prism   pentagonal prism   hexagonal prism

Note that each prism takes its name from the polygon that forms two of its faces.

A **pyramid** has one base in the shape of a polygon. It has triangular faces which meet at a point at the top called the **apex**.

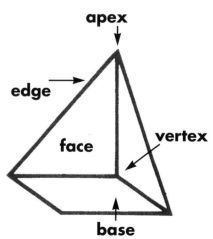

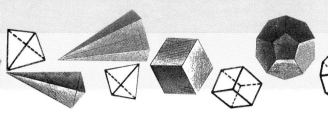

geometric solids

Geometric solids with polygons for faces are called
polyhedrons. **Poly** and **hedron** are ancient
Greek words meaning *many* and *face*.

The five **Platonic solids** make up a special set
of polyhedrons. These polyhedrons are special
because they are the only solids with faces that
are regular congruent polygons.

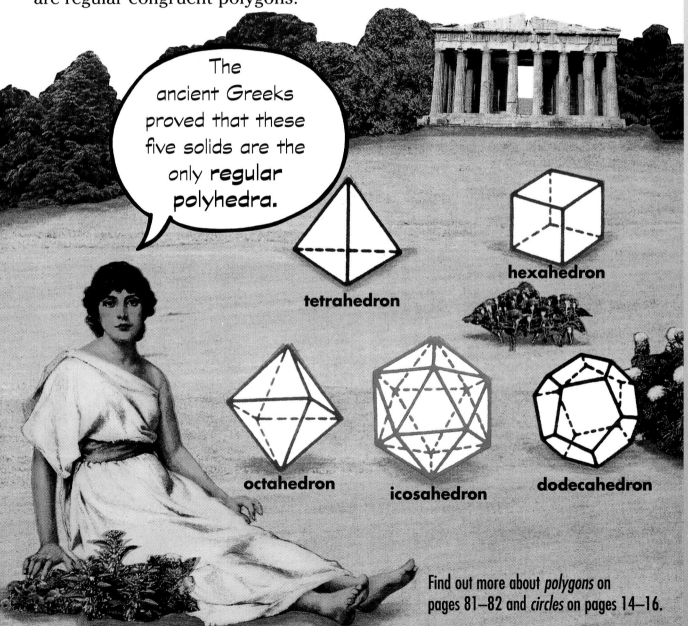

The ancient Greeks proved that these five solids are the only **regular polyhedra.**

tetrahedron

hexahedron

octahedron

icosahedron

dodecahedron

Find out more about *polygons* on
pages 81–82 and *circles* on pages 14–16.

Inequality

An **inequality** is a comparison in which two quantities are not the same. The symbols for *greater than* (**>**) and *less than* (**<**) are used to show an inequality.

Note that the point of the inequality symbol always points to the smaller number or expression.

8 > 5

(2 + 4) < (3 + 5)

11 > 6

11 is greater than 6.

Integers

Integers include whole numbers and their opposites, where zero is its own opposite. The numbers greater than zero are called **positive numbers**, and the numbers less than zero are called **negative numbers**.

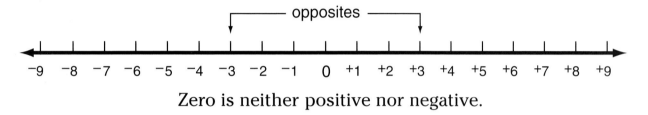

opposites

−9 −8 −7 −6 −5 −4 −3 −2 −1 0 +1 +2 +3 +4 +5 +6 +7 +8 +9

Zero is neither positive nor negative.

Sometimes we rate things positively or negatively.

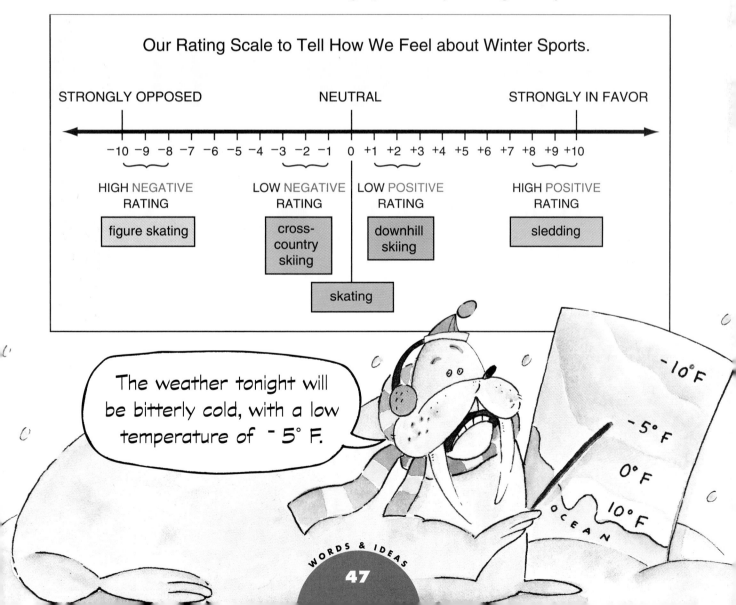

Our Rating Scale to Tell How We Feel about Winter Sports.

STRONGLY OPPOSED   NEUTRAL   STRONGLY IN FAVOR

−10 −9 −8 −7 −6 −5 −4 −3 −2 −1 0 +1 +2 +3 +4 +5 +6 +7 +8 +9 +10

HIGH NEGATIVE RATING — figure skating

LOW NEGATIVE RATING — cross-country skiing

LOW POSITIVE RATING — downhill skiing

HIGH POSITIVE RATING — sledding

skating

The weather tonight will be bitterly cold, with a low temperature of ⁻5° F.

−10°F
−5°F
0°F
10°F
OCEAN

WORDS & IDEAS

47

Length

The **length (linear measure)** is the measure of distance from one end of an object to the other end.

Find out more about *length* on pages 122–123.

A **line** is a set of points that extends endlessly in opposite directions. Usually we mean a **straight line** when we use the term *line*.

This is the symbol for this line. $\overleftrightarrow{AB}$

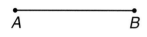

A **line segment** is a part of a line that lies between two given points. These two points are called **endpoints**.

This is the symbol for this line segment. $\overline{AB}$

A **ray** is part of a line that has only one endpoint.

This is the symbol for this ray. $\overrightarrow{AB}$

Lines that **intersect** are lines that cross each other.

Two lines that intersect at a **90°** angle (a right angle) are called **perpendicular lines**.

This is the symbol for this pair of perpendicular lines. $\overline{AB} \perp \overline{CD}$

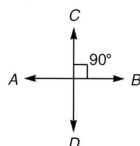

lines

If two lines in a plane do not intersect, they are called **parallel lines**. Two parallel lines are a fixed distance apart.

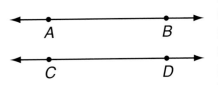

This is the symbol for this pair of parallel lines. $\overline{AB} \parallel \overline{CD}$

Skew lines are not parallel and do not intersect.

| parallel lines | intersecting lines | skew lines | perpendicular lines |

Logical Reasoning

Logical reasoning is thinking in an organized way. We can use logical reasoning to solve logic problems.

Making charts and diagrams often helps us understand clues. We can use logical reasoning to create a chart to solve this problem.

Name ———————————— Date ————

Who has which pet?

Romunda, Maria, and Nate each have a different pet. Their pets are a dog, a cat, and a hamster.

Maria's pet is not a hamster. Romunda wishes that her pet were a dog. Nate's pet likes to catch mice.

	dog	cat	hamster
Romunda	No	No	Yes
Maria	Yes	No	No
Nate	No	Yes	No

Name ———————————— Date ————

There are 12 students.

7 students like cats.

9 students like dogs.

How many students like both cats and dogs?

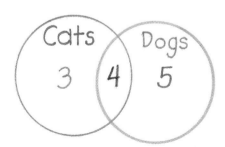

7 + 9 = 16 votes in all.
16 - 12 = 4 students voted for both.

Venn diagrams help us visualize information in a logical way. We can use words such as *all*, *every*, *some*, *none*, *not all*, *both*, and *only* to describe logical reasoning in a Venn diagram.

We can use logical reasoning to solve this problem by creating a Venn diagram.

We can see from the diagram that 4 students liked both cats and dogs.

A **map** is a picture that tells us where we can find objects and places. When we look at a map we see the objects on it or the landscape from a "bird's eye view."

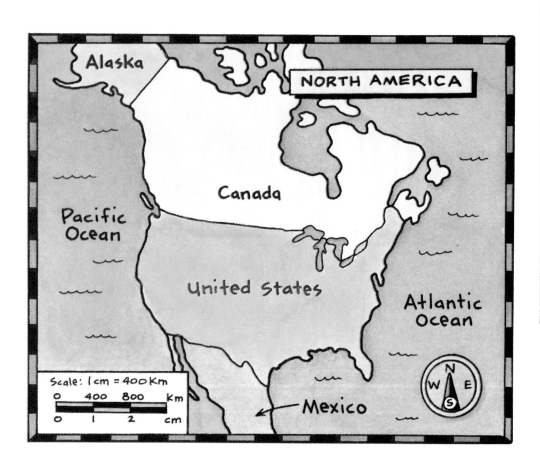

Usually there is a **scale** on a map. The scale helps us find the distance between locations.

On the map of North America the scale is 1 centimeter to 400 kilometers. This tells us that each centimeter represents 400 kilometers.

To find out how far it is from one place to another, we measure how many centimeters the two places are apart on the map, and then multiply by **400**.

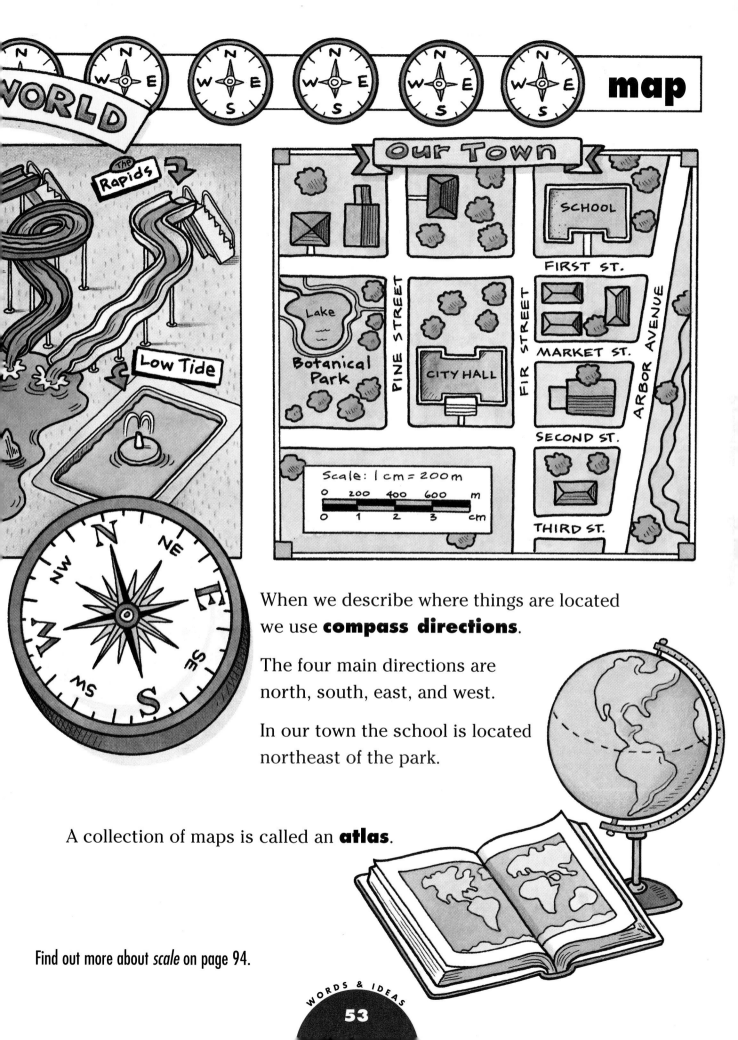

map

WORLD

The Rapids

Low Tide

Our Town

SCHOOL

FIRST ST.

PINE STREET

FIR STREET

ARBOR AVENUE

Lake

Botanical
Park

CITY HALL

MARKET ST.

SECOND ST.

Scale: 1 cm = 200m

0   200   400   600   m

0   1   2   3   cm

THIRD ST.

When we describe where things are located
we use **compass directions**.

The four main directions are
north, south, east, and west.

In our town the school is located
northeast of the park.

A collection of maps is called an **atlas**.

Find out more about *scale* on page 94.

WORDS & IDEAS

53

Mass

Mass is the measure of the amount of matter contained by an object. Grams and kilograms are units of mass.

Although most people use the terms *mass* and *weight* interchangeably, scientists use the words to mean slightly different things. **Weight** is a measure of the force gravity exerts on a mass. At sea level, measures of mass and weight are equal.

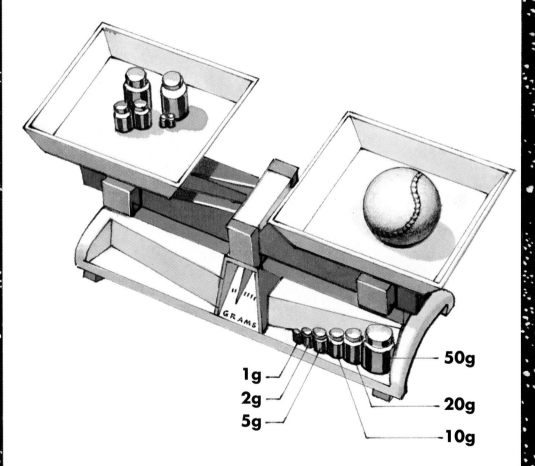

1g
2g
5g
50g
20g
10g

The mass of the baseball is 144 grams.

Mean

The **mean**, often called the **average**, is a number that summarizes a set of data. To find the mean, add all of the numbers in a data set, and then divide the sum by the number of items in the set.

Here is how Terry figured his mean score (bowling average).

115 + 139 + 127 = 381

381 ÷ 3 = 127

Terry's mean score was **127**. We might also say that Terry bowled an average of **127** pins.

The mean can also tell us what is typical about a data set. This can help us make predictions.

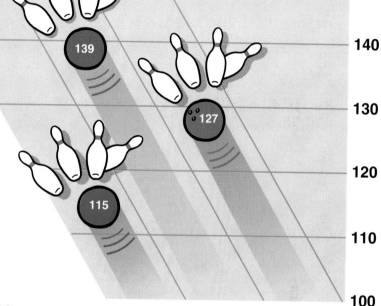

Bowling
Scores

Latisha experimented with raisins. First she found that the mean number of raisins in the boxes was **35**. Then Latisha predicted that a new raisin box would contain about **35** raisins.

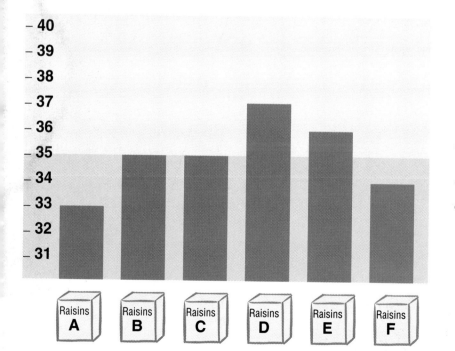

Find out more about *averages* on pages 10 – 11 and *statistics* on pages 98 – 99.

Measurement

In many situations in our everyday lives we need to **measure** something or find its **dimensions**.

When we need to know how far, how long, how tall or how wide something is, we find the **distance**, **length**, **height**, or **width**.

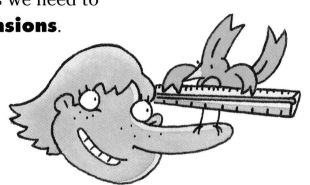

When we need to know how heavy or light something is, we find the **weight**.

When we need to know how much liquid something can hold, we find the **capacity**.

Sometimes we need to know how hot or cold something is. Then we find the **temperature**.

When we need to know how long something takes, we measure **time**.

There are two different systems of measurement: the customary system and the metric system.

The amount or quantity used as a standard of measurement is called a **unit**. When an object is measured, we use labels to show which units were used to measure the object.

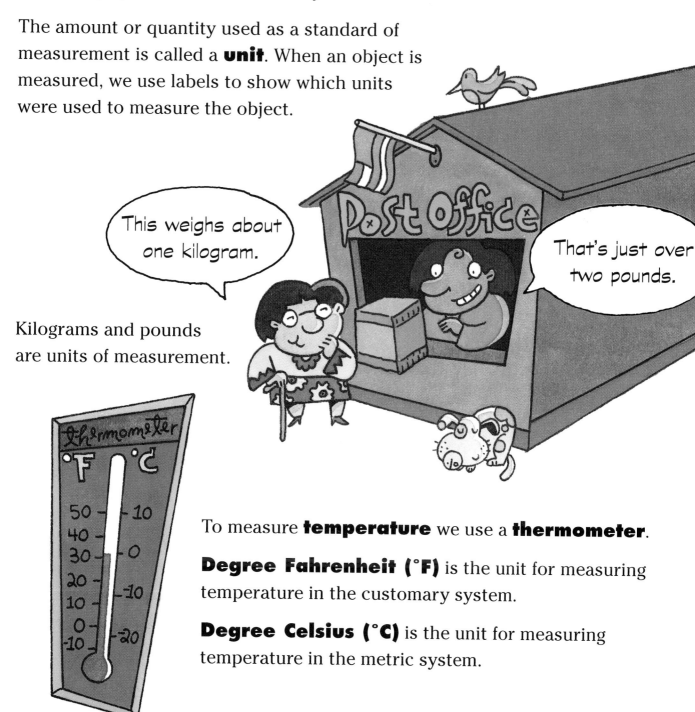

This weighs about one kilogram.

That's just over two pounds.

Kilograms and pounds are units of measurement.

To measure **temperature** we use a **thermometer**.

Degree Fahrenheit (°F) is the unit for measuring temperature in the customary system.

Degree Celsius (°C) is the unit for measuring temperature in the metric system.

Find out more about *measurement equivalencies* on pages 121–128.

Median

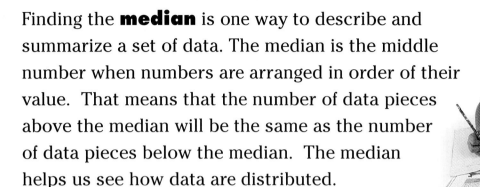

Finding the **median** is one way to describe and summarize a set of data. The median is the middle number when numbers are arranged in order of their value. That means that the number of data pieces above the median will be the same as the number of data pieces below the median. The median helps us see how data are distributed.

This line plot shows the number of hours a group of fifth graders spent on homework for a week.

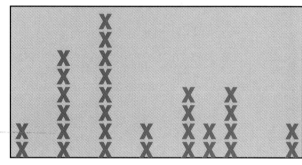

```
                        X
            X           X
            X           X
            X           X            X     X
            X           X            X     X
  X         X           X      X     X  X  X        X
  X         X           X      X     X  X  X        X
  2  3  4   5   6  7  8  9  10 11 12 13 14 15
```

Here is one way to find the median.
Count the number of data along the line plot.
Here we have **30** pieces of data.

2 2 4 4 4 4 4 4 6 6 6 6 6 6 6 | 6 8 8 10 10 10 10 11 11 12 12 12 12 15 15

⎣_____15_____⎦ ↑Median ⎣_____15_____⎦

To figure out the center of the data we divide **30** by **2** and get **15**. Next we find the fifteenth number by counting from each side of the line plot. Because we have an even number of data the middle or median is between two numbers.

The median for this set of data is **6**. That means that about half the group spent **6** or less hours on homework, and about half the group spent **6** or more hours on homework.

Find out more about *data* on pages 21 and *statistics* on pages 98–99.

Finding the **mode** is one way that we summarize and describe data. The mode is the number that occurs most often in a set of data.

There can be more than one mode if there are two or more numbers that occur the same number of times.

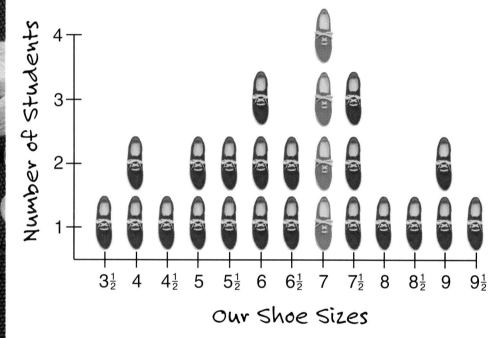

The mode for this set of data is 7.

Find out more about *data* on page 21 and *statistics* on pages 98–99.

Money

Money is something we trade to get something else.
Currency is the name used to describe the different kinds of coins and bills traded in different countries.

This is the currency used in the United States.

penny
one cent
1¢

nickel
five cents
5¢

dime
ten cents
10¢

quarter
twenty-five cents
25¢

half-dollar
fifty cents
50¢

one-dollar bill
one dollar
$1

five-dollar bill
five dollars
$5

ten-dollar bill
ten dollars
$10

twenty-dollar bill
twenty dollars
$20

INTERNATIONAL
CURRENCY
EXCHANGE

fifty-dollar bill
fifty dollars
$50

hundred-dollar bill
one hundred dollars
$100

Please change
my Indian rupee for
dollars.

Here is the currency used in Canada.

penny
one cent
1¢

nickel
five cents
5¢

dime
ten cents
10¢

quarter
twenty-five cents
25¢

half dollar
fifty cents
50¢

one-dollar coin (loonie)
one dollar
$1

two-dollar bill
two dollars
$2

five-dollar bill
five dollars
$5

How many dollars for my Canadian dollars?

I need yen to use in Japan.

I'm going to Mexico, so I'll need some pesos.

ten-dollar bill
ten dollars
$10

twenty-dollar bill
twenty dollars
$20

I need to exchange my Korean won for dollars.

fifty-dollar bill
fifty dollars
$50

hundred-dollar bill
one hundred dollars
$100

Motion Geometry

Motion geometry compares shapes before and after they are moved or transformed in space.

Three basic motions are **slides (translations)**, **turns (rotations)**, and **flips (reflections)**. When these motions are used, lengths, angles, and areas of shapes are not changed.

A **slide** or **translation** is when a shape is moved to another position without turning or flipping.

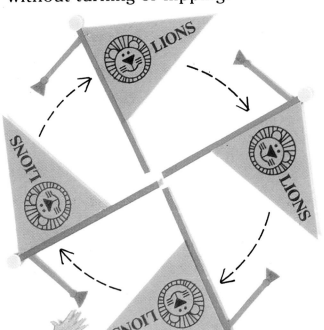

A **turn** or **rotation** is when a shape is moved around any given fixed point.

A **flip** or **reflection** is when a shape is a mirror image.

Multiplication

Multiplication is an operation we use to *combine equal groups*.

I can multiply to find the total because they are equal groups.

I have to add to find the total because the groups are not equal.

Sometimes it is helpful to view equal groups as an **array**.

An array is an arrangement of equal groups in rows and columns.

3 x 4

4

3

3 x 24

24

3

13 x 24

24

13

There are special names and symbols we use for multiplication.

factor

product

factor →

$$32 \times 5 = 160$$

multiplication sign

equal sign

There are different ways to multiply.

32 x 5 = ?

Sometimes I can do the multiplication in my head.

I'll break it into a smaller problem.

I know 3 times 5 is 15, then I add a 0 because the 3 is actually 30.

Then I take 2 times 5, which is 10.

Now I add 150 and 10 and I get 160.

32 times 5 is 160.

GRRROINK

23 × 12

I'll find this product using a calculator.

First I'll estimate.

I know 23 times 12 is about 20 times 10, which is 200.

The product should be about 200.

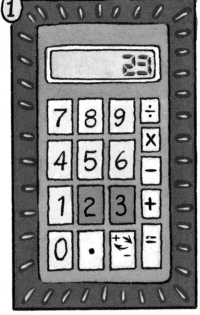

THAT'S A LOT OF FRENCH FRIES!

Multiplication and addition are related.

5 x 23 is the same as **5** groups of **23**,

or **23 + 23 + 23 + 23 + 23**.

Multiplication and division are also related.

Because **23 x 12 = 276**, we can divide **276**
into the same parts.

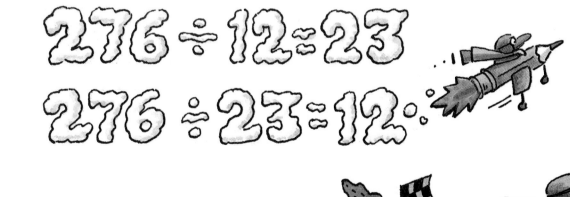

Negative Numbers

Negative numbers and positive numbers are opposites. The value of a negative number is **less than 0** and the value of a positive number is **greater than 0**.

$^-6$ $^-4$ $^-2$ 0 $^+2$ $^+4$ $^+6$

⁻4 and 4 are opposites. Both numbers are 4 units away from 0 in opposite directions.

Negative numbers are useful in many situations.

The temperature is 4 degrees below 0 or ⁻4°.

Squid like to live about 400 meters below sea level, or ⁻400 m.

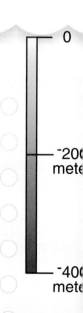

A **net** is a two-dimensional picture of a three-dimensional figure.

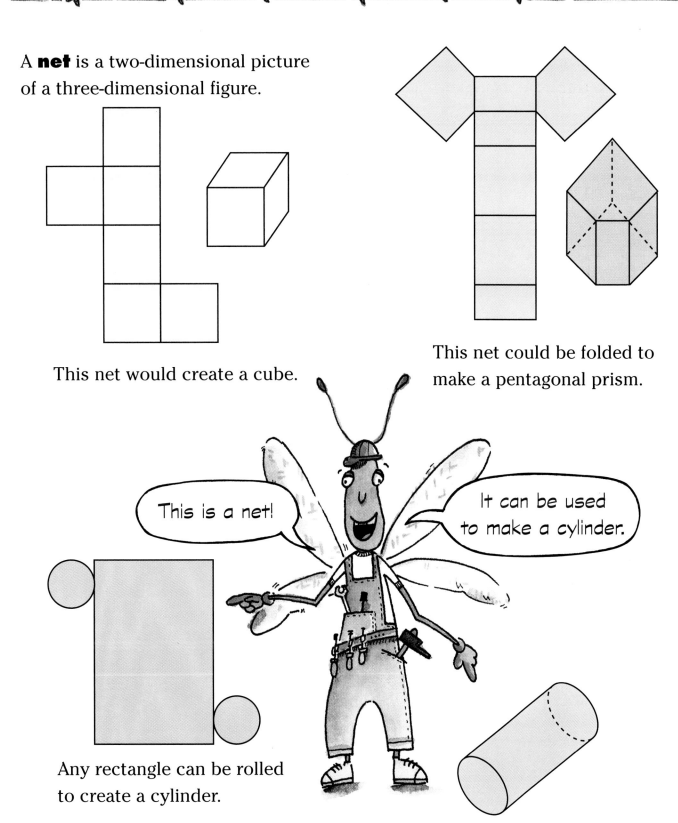

This net would create a cube.

This net could be folded to make a pentagonal prism.

This is a net!

It can be used to make a cylinder.

Any rectangle can be rolled to create a cylinder.

Find out more about *three-dimensional figures* on pages 43–45.

Numbers

A **number** is an idea that tells how many.

A **numeral** is a symbol for a number.

Our number system uses ten **digits**. The digits are 0, 1, 2, 3, 4, 5, 6, 7, 8, and 9.

When we want to describe a group of numbers, we say they belong to a **set**. A set of numbers is always shown with a curly bracket { } on each side.

Counting numbers are the numbers greater than zero.

{1, 2, 3, 4, ...}

Whole numbers are the counting numbers and zero.

{0, 1, 2, 3, 4, ...}

Integers are the counting numbers, their opposites, and zero.

{ ..., −4, −3, −2, −1, 0, 1, 2, 3, 4, ... }

An **even number** is any whole number that is a multiple of **2**. The ones digit of an even number is **0, 2, 4, 6,** or **8**.

Some even Numbers
10
22
266
2,718

An **odd number** is any whole number that is not an even number. The ones digit of an odd number is **1, 3, 5, 7,** or **9**.

Some odd Numbers
11
23
267
2,719

3 1 4 9 8 2 2 4 9 3 5

A **number line** is a line that shows numbers in order.

-4 -3 -2 -1 0 1 2 3 4 5 6 7 8 9 10 11 12

I am second in line.

An **ordinal number** is a number that is used to describe order. Some ordinal numbers are first, third, and tenth.

Jane was born on the fifth of June.

JUNE 5

Each piece is one eighth.

We use ordinal numbers when we write fractions in words.

Negative numbers are the integers that are less than zero.

$$\{..., ^-3, ^-2, ^-1\}$$

Positive numbers are the integers that are greater than zero.

$$\{1, 2, 3, ...\}$$

Rational numbers are numbers that can be expressed as a quotient of two integers.

$\frac{2}{5}$ and $\frac{^-3}{4}$ are examples of rational numbers.

numbers

A **square number** is the product of a number multiplied by itself.

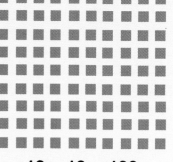

2 x 2 = 4
Four is
a square number.

3 x 3 = 9
Nine is a
square number.

10 x 10 = 100
One hundred
is a square number.

Triangular numbers form an addition pattern.

1

1 + 2 = 3

1 + 2 + 3 = 6

1 + 2 + 3 + 4 = 10

A **googol** is the number **1** followed by **100** zeros.

1,000,000,000

1 billion

1,000,000

1 million

10,000,000,000,000,000,000,
000,000,000,000,000,000,000,
000,000,000,000,000,000,000,
000,000,000,000,000,000,000,
000,000,000,000, 000,000

1 googol

Find out about *prime numbers* on page 83 and *composite numbers* on page 17.

Order of Operations

Sometimes we need to solve problems that use more than one operation. The answer we get may depend on the order in which we do the operations. To get exactly one solution, we must follow rules about the order in which we do the operations.

This is the **Order of Operations**:

Compute inside **P**arentheses first.

Compute the **E**xponents next.

Do all **M**ultiplications and **D**ivisions next, left to right.

Do all **A**dditions and **S**ubtractions last, left to right.

We can use the saying "**P**lease **E**xcuse **M**y **D**ear **A**unt **S**ally" to remember the order of operations.

Please
Excuse
My
Dear
Aunt
Sally

$(10-3) \times (5+2) = ?$

I'll follow the order of operations.

10 - 3 = 7
and 5 + 2 = 7

That's 7 × 7 = 49.

Pattern

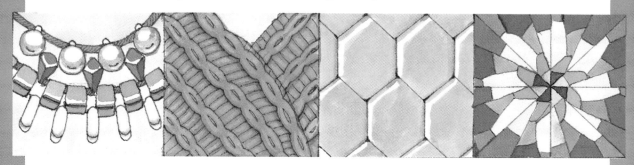

A **pattern** is a sequence of objects, events, or ideas that repeat. The number of different patterns to be found are unlimited. Much of a mathematician's work is searching for patterns.

Here are some patterns defined by shape.

Here are some number patterns.

5, **10**, **15**, **20**, **25**, ... counting forward by fives

100, **98**, **96**, **94**, **92**, **90**, ... counting backward by twos

A thirteenth century Italian mathematician, Leonardo Fibonacci, noticed that there are patterns in nature. He discovered a number series to describe these patterns, known as the **Fibonacci numbers**.

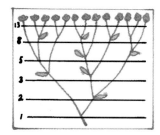

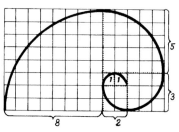

Here are Fibonacci's numbers.

1, **1**, **2**, **3**, **5**, **8**, **13**, **21**, **34**, **55**, **89**, ...

Blaise Pascal was a French mathematician who lived during the 1600s. Pascal created a triangular pattern of numbers. This pattern is sometimes used to determine the probability of combinations.

Row	Pascal's Triangle
0	1
1	1 1
2	1 2 1
3	1 3 3 1
4	1 4 6 4 1

Here are some patterns we see in **Pascal's triangle**.

Each row begins and ends with a one.

To find a number in the pattern we add the numbers that are directly right and left in the row above.

Here is a growth pattern. This pattern grows step by step.

  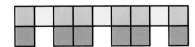

step 1   **step 2**   **step 3**

Percent

10% OFF ADMISSION **10% OFF ADMISSION** **10% OFF ADMISSION**

Percent is a special kind of ratio or fraction where the denominator is **100**. The word *percent* is short for the Latin *per centum*, meaning *by the hundred*. The symbol for percent is **%**.

The grid shows that **45** out of **100** squares are shaded and **55** out of **100** are not shaded.

For the shaded part we can write:

fraction		decimal		percent
$\frac{45}{100}$	=	0.45	=	45%

For the unshaded part we can write:

fraction		decimal		percent
$\frac{55}{100}$	=	0.55	=	55%

We read **45%** as "forty-five percent."

We read **55%** as "fifty-five percent."

These are the same!

50% OFF

HOT DOGS

$\frac{1}{2}$ OFF

We use some percents quite often.

$\frac{1}{2} = 50\%$ $\frac{3}{4} = 75\%$ $\frac{1}{5} = 20\%$ $\frac{1}{4} = 25\%$ $\frac{1}{3} = 33\frac{1}{3}\%$

Percents can help us make comparisons. Sometimes in order to compare quantities we have to convert a fraction or a decimal to a percent. Here are two ways to convert a fraction to a percent.

One way to convert a fraction to a percent is to write and solve a proportion.

$$\frac{4}{5} = \frac{?}{100}$$

Think: **4** is to **5** as what number is to **100**?

$$\frac{4}{5} = \frac{80}{100}$$

Since **5** multiplied by **20** is **100**, we multiply the numerator by **20** also. The product is **80**.

So, $\frac{4}{5}$ = **80%**

Another way to convert a fraction to a percent is to divide the numerator by the denominator.

$\frac{5}{8}$ means **5 ÷ 8 = 0.625**

Move the decimal point two places to the right to write the percent.

0.625 = 62.5%

So, $\frac{5}{8}$ = **62.5%**

80% is greater than **62.5%**, so **4** out of **5** is better than **5** out of **8**.

Perimeter

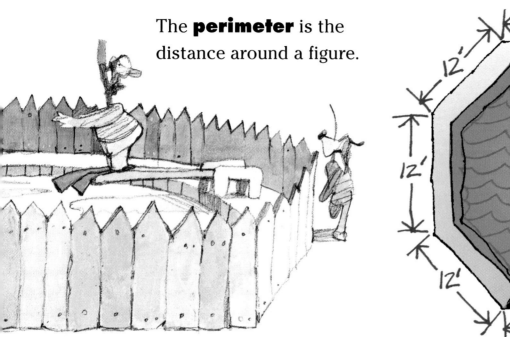

The **perimeter** is the distance around a figure.

12 + 12 + 12 + 12 + 12 + 12 + 12 + 12 = 96 feet

p = **96** feet

The distance around a circle is called the **circumference**.

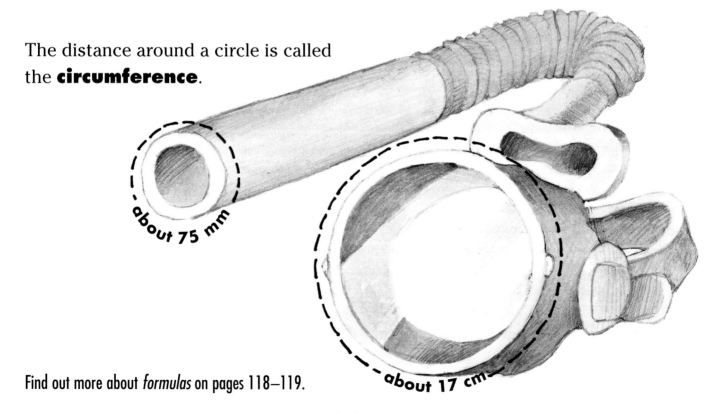

about 75 mm

about 17 cm

Find out more about *formulas* on pages 118–119.

Place Value

A **numeration system** is a plan for recording numbers.

We record numbers using the **Hindu-Arabic** numeration system. We use the **digits** **0**, **1**, **2**, **3**, **4**, **5**, **6**, **7**, **8**, **9**. In our numeration system we group by tens.

The position or place of a digit in a number tells the value of that digit. This is called **place value**.

We group digits to help us read large numbers. The groups are called **periods**.

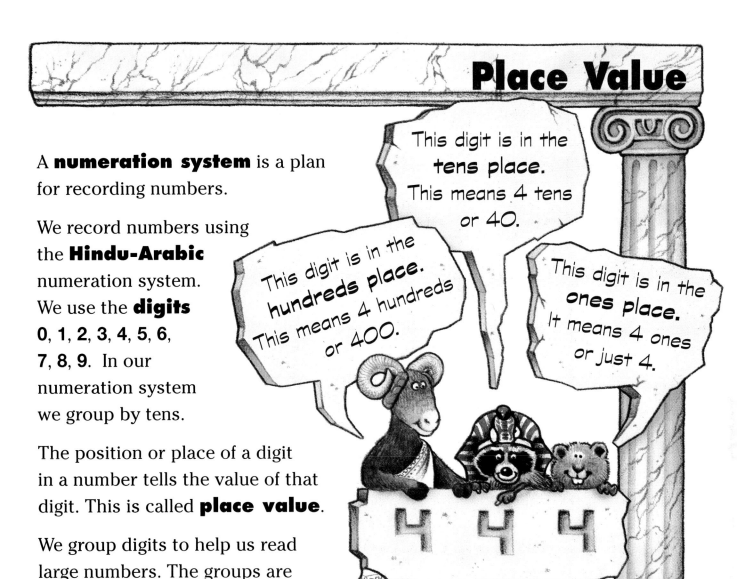

This digit is in the **tens place**. This means 4 tens or 40.

This digit is in the **hundreds place**. This means 4 hundreds or 400.

This digit is in the **ones place**. It means 4 ones or just 4.

Periods	Billions			Millions			Thousands			Ones		
Place Values	hundred billions	ten billions	billions	hundred millions	ten millions	millions	hundred thousands	ten thousands	thousands	hundreds	tens	ones
	2	3	8,	1	2	7,	6	5	3,	9	4	1

We read this number as two hundred thirty-eight **billion**, one hundred twenty-seven **million**, six hundred fifty-three **thousand**, nine hundred forty-one.

place value

We can also use place value to describe the parts of a number less than one.

We read this number as **one thousand four and eight hundred seventy-five thousandths.**

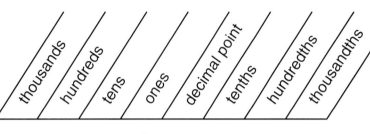

thousands | hundreds | tens | ones | decimal point | tenths | hundredths | thousandths

1, 0   0   4 . 8   7   5

↑
decimal point

CDXCVI
496

Roman numerals are also a numeration system.

I = 1   V = 5   X = 10   L = 50

C = 100   D = 500   M = 1,000

Here are some examples of large and small numbers.

**2,400,000
2.4 million**

**125,000
125 thousand**

**0.67
sixty-seven hundredths**

**0.003
three thousandths**

Polygon

A **polygon** is a closed figure formed by line segments.

These are polygons.

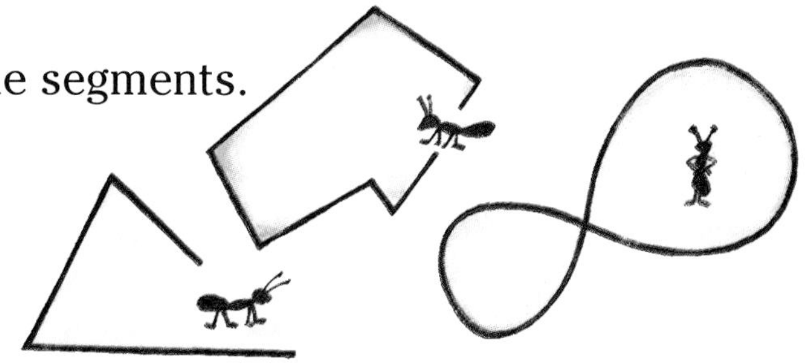

These are not polygons.

A **regular polygon** has equal sides and equal angles.

This is a regular polygon.

This is an irregular polygon.

Each line segment of a polygon is called a **side**.

A point where two sides meet is called a **vertex**. The plural of vertex is **vertices**. A line that joins two opposite vertices is called a **diagonal** of the polygon.

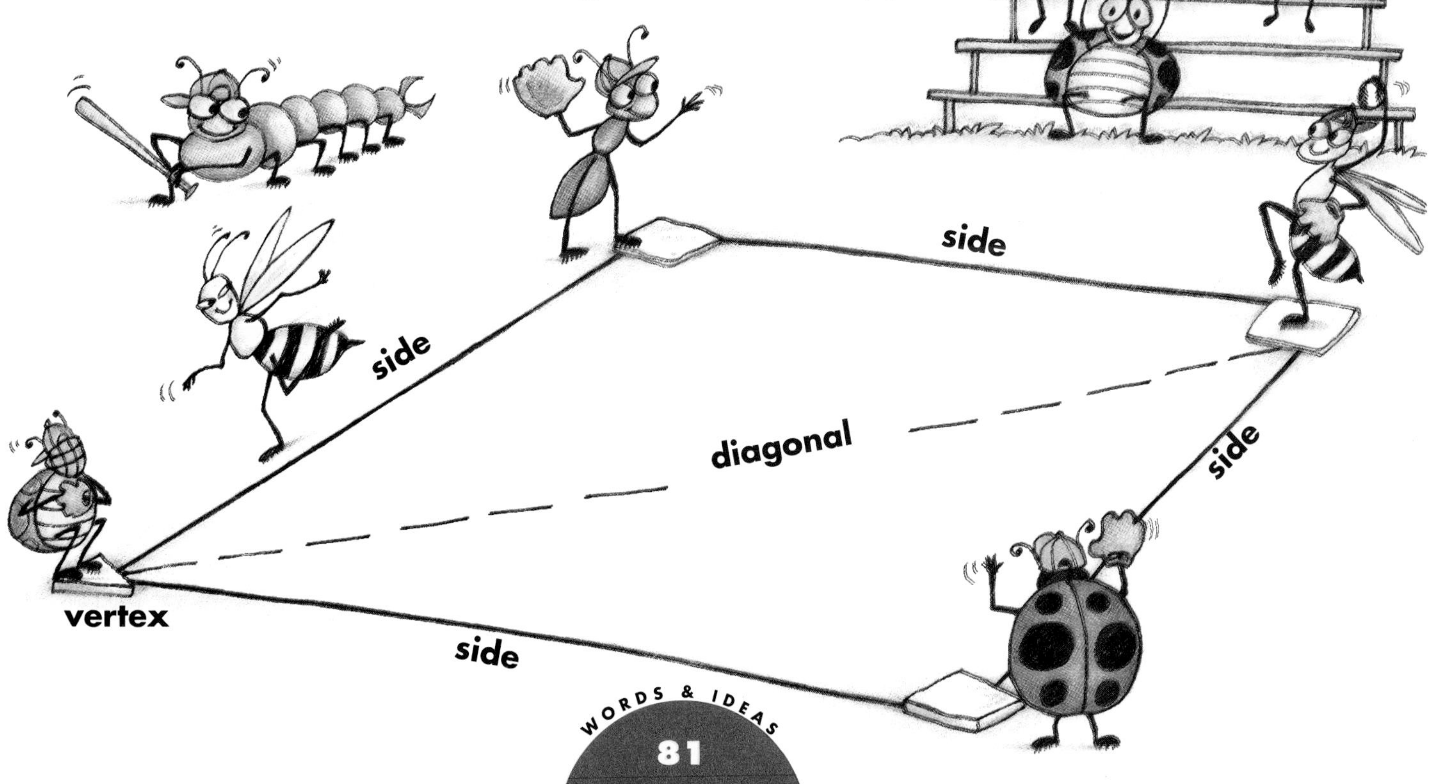

side

side

diagonal

side

vertex

side

polygon

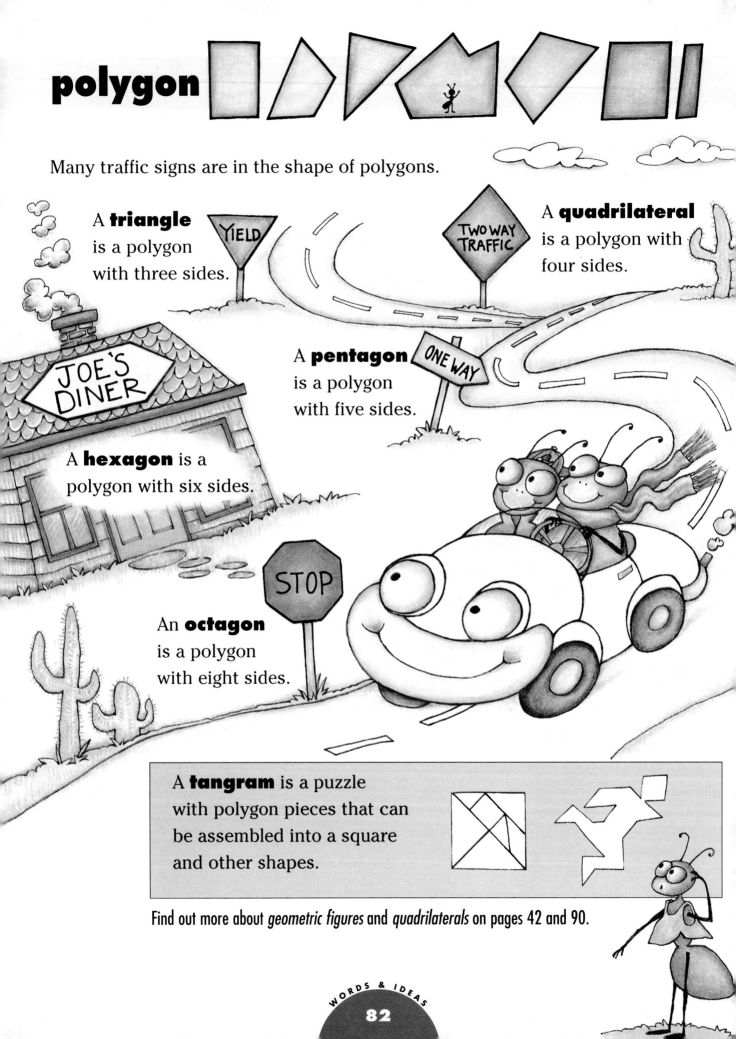

Many traffic signs are in the shape of polygons.

A **triangle** is a polygon with three sides.

YIELD

A **quadrilateral** is a polygon with four sides.

TWO WAY TRAFFIC

A **pentagon** is a polygon with five sides.

ONE WAY

JOE'S DINER

A **hexagon** is a polygon with six sides.

STOP

An **octagon** is a polygon with eight sides.

A **tangram** is a puzzle with polygon pieces that can be assembled into a square and other shapes.

Find out more about *geometric figures* and *quadrilaterals* on pages 42 and 90.

A **prime number** is a number that has only two factors, itself and the number 1.

A prime number cannot be expressed as a product of two smaller numbers. Therefore it cannot be displayed in an array with more than one row.

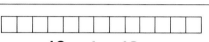

2 = 1 x 2
Two has only 2 factors.
Two is a prime number.

13 = 1 x 13
Thirteen has only 2 factors.
Thirteen is a prime number.

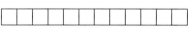

12 = 1 x 12

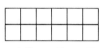

12 = 2 x 6

12 = 3 x 4

Twelve has 6 factors. It is a **composite number**.

All numbers that are greater than 1, and are not prime, are **composite numbers**.

When we express a composite number as a product of prime factors, we write the **prime factorization** of a number.

$$12 = 2 \times 2 \times 3$$

prime factors

Here are the prime numbers less than **30**.

2, 3, 5, 7, 11, 13, 17, 19, 23, 29

> The number 1 is neither prime nor composite.

Find out more about *composite numbers* on page 17.

Probability

Probability is the study of chance. Ideas related to probability are involved in many parts of our lives. Understanding probability can help us make better decisions.

We often use words such as *likely* and *unlikely* to talk about ideas of probability in everyday situations. Mathematics helps us be more specific about probability. We can assign a number to the probability of something happening.

The **probability of an event** is the ratio of the number of ways an event can occur to the total number of possible outcomes.

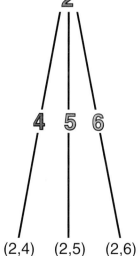

We'll toss this coin 100 times. The outcomes are heads or tails.

Since two outcomes are possible, we would expect to get heads **50** times out of the **100** tosses.

The probability of getting heads can be expressed

$$P \text{ (heads)} = \frac{50}{100}$$

The **mathematical or theoretical probability** is $\frac{50}{100}$. It tells us what we can expect the outcome to be over a large number of trials.

A **tree diagram** helps determine probability by showing the number of equally likely outcomes.

If we spin both spinners we get a pair of numbers as an outcome. This tree diagram shows all possible outcomes.

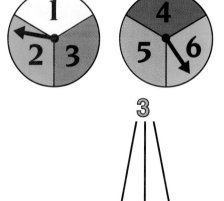

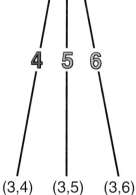

First Spinner	1			2			3		
Second Spinner	4	5	6	4	5	6	4	5	6
Outcomes	(1,4)	(1,5)	(1,6)	(2,4)	(2,5)	(2,6)	(3,4)	(3,5)	(3,6)

There are nine equally likely outcomes.

Problem Solving

We can use many different ways or **strategies** to solve problems. The strategies we choose will depend on the type of problem. We can learn more about different strategies when we ask people how they solve problems.

Here are some common strategies we might use.

Sometimes we can **act out** or move objects to help us solve a problem.

Bob is third in line. Jane is not last, and she is behind Ann. Peter is not first. Who is last?

Line starts here

PETER BOB JANE ANN

If it is difficult to act out a problem, we might **make a diagram** or picture to help us.

The cat climbed 6 feet up the tree.

Then it climbed down 2 feet.

Then it climbed up another 6 feet.

Sometimes the best way to solve a problem is to **choose an operation**. In order to determine whether you should add, subtract, multiply, or divide, you need to understand the problem. Sometimes it helps to rewrite the problem in your own words.

If you earn $15.00 a week doing chores, how many weeks will it take you to earn $125.00 for new skates?

How many weeks will it take to earn $125.00 if I earn $15.00 each week?

BOB

I need to divide 125 by 15.

Sometimes we might **make an organized list** to find the number of possible combinations.

• POSSIBLE COMBINATIONS
Gray shirt — Denim pants / Black pants
White Shirt — Denim pants / Black pants
Blue Shirt — Denim pants / Black pants

How many trees will we plant to earn about $500.00?

1	2	3	4	5	6	7	8	9	10	11
1	2	4	8	16	32	64	128	256	512	

If there are a number of possible solutions, we might **create a table** or **look for a pattern**.

The amount of money doubles each time we plant a tree.

problem solving

Adam scored 24 points on a ten-question history test. The test had 2-point and 3-point questions.

How many of each kind of question did Adam answer correctly?

Sometimes we can solve a problem by **guessing** a number and then **checking** our guess.

If he answered five 2-point questions and five 3-point questions tha would be too many points

Let's try six 2-point questions and four 3-point questions.

That works!

Sometimes it is helpful to start at the end of a problem and **work backward** by reversing the actions to find the solution.

How long is the snake?

If you subtract 12 from its length and then double that difference you will get 34.

I'll take 34 and divide by 2 instead of doubling.

Then I'll add 12 instead of subtracting.

The snake is 29 inches. That seems reasonable!

$$34 \div 2 = 17$$
$$17 + 12 = 29$$

We use **ratios** to describe proportion. A **proportion** is a statement that two ratios are equal.

We can use proportional thinking to solve problems.

> I weigh about 75 pounds. I wonder how much of my weight is muscle?

For each 5 pounds of your body weight, about 2 pounds is muscle.

A proportion can compare two different quantities measured in the same unit. In this problem we compare muscle weight in pounds to body weight in pounds.

$$\frac{\textbf{muscle weight}}{\textbf{body weight}} = \frac{2}{5} = \frac{?}{75}$$

Since **5 x 15 = 75**, we can multiply **2** by **15**.

$$\frac{2 \times 15}{5 \times 15} = \frac{30}{75}$$

Her muscle weight is **30** pounds.

Find out more about *ratio* on pages 91–92.

Quadrilaterals

Polygons with four sides can be called **quadrilaterals**.

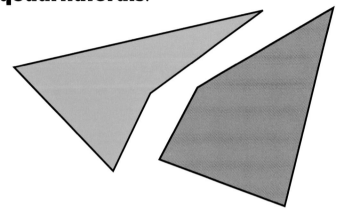

A **square** is a quadrilateral that has four right angles and four equal sides.

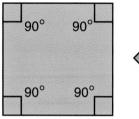

A **rhombus** is a quadrilateral with opposite sides parallel and all sides equal.

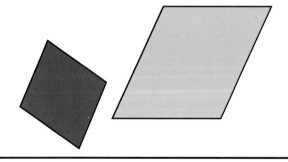

A **rectangle** is a quadrilateral that has four right angles and has opposite sides of equal length.

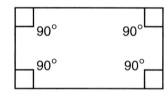

A **trapezoid** is a quadrilateral with only two parallel sides.

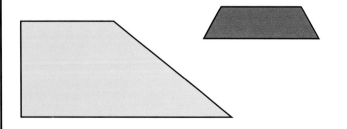

A **parallelogram** is a quadrilateral with opposite sides parallel and equal. A square, rectangle, and rhombus are examples of parallelograms.

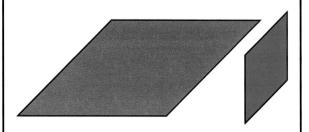

Ratio

A **ratio** is a comparison of two quantities.

One type of ratio compares one group to another group.

We can write the ratio of penguins to polar bears in three ways:

with words	**4 to 6**
with a colon	**4:6**
as a fraction	$\frac{4}{6}$

Another type of ratio compares a part to a whole.

Here are five pairs of shoes.

Two pairs are sneakers.

We can write the ratio of pairs of sneakers to total pairs of shoes as

2 to **5** or **2:5** or $\frac{2}{5}$.

A third type of ratio compares one quantity or amount to another that is measured in a different unit. This is called a **rate**. We see many different types of rates.

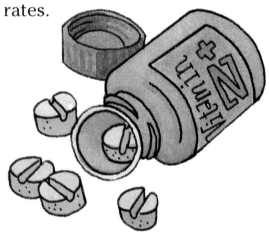

4 pills per day means $\dfrac{4 \text{ pills}}{1 \text{ day}}$ **or 4 to 1.**

75 km/h means $\dfrac{75 \text{ km}}{1 \text{ h}}$ **or 75 to 1.**

Ratios can be simplified.

3 tickets cost **$6**. This can be written as the ratio **3:6**.

3:6 can be simplified to **1:2**. This means **1** ticket costs **$2**.

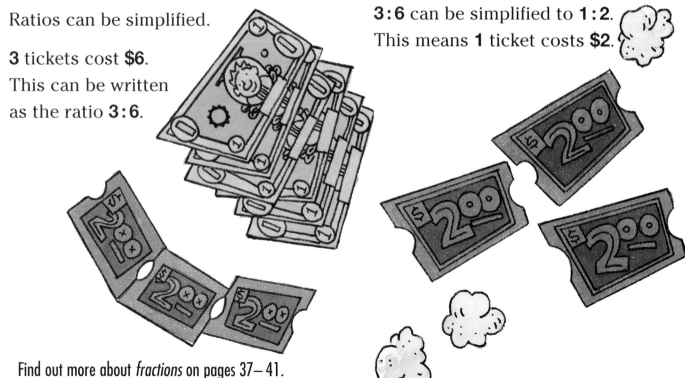

Find out more about *fractions* on pages 37–41.

When we want to find information about a very large group of data, but we cannot actually gather that large group of data, we can use a sample. A **sample** is a smaller group that shares the characteristics of the larger group. The larger group is called the **population**. **Sampling** is the process of gathering information from the sample to make predictions about the population.

If you wanted to know if the students in your school would support a recycling program, you might ask the students in your class and then make a prediction. The sample is the students in your class. The population is the students in the entire school. Sampling is the collecting of data for one class.

> We found that three-fourths of the students in our class want to help recycle at school.

> So we predict that a recycling program would be supported by most students in the entire school.

Find out more about *statistics* on pages 98—99.

Scale

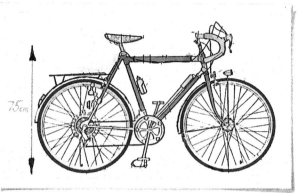

When objects and pictures are too large or too small to draw to their actual size, we make a **scale drawing**.

The **scale** for the drawing tells how the drawing compares to the original object.

What is the height of the scale drawing of the bike? We can use the scale and the actual measurement to find the missing information. The height of the scale drawing is **7.5** cm.

$$\frac{1 \text{ cm}}{10 \text{ cm}} = \frac{?}{75 \text{ cm}}$$

$$\frac{1 \text{ cm}}{10 \text{ cm}} = \frac{7.5 \text{ cm}}{75 \text{ cm}}$$

Changing the scale of one measurement for an object changes other measurements for the object.

Actual Length

volume of cube =
1 x 1 x 1 =
1 cubic cm

Double the Scale Length

volume of cube =
2 x 2 x 2 =
8 cubic cm

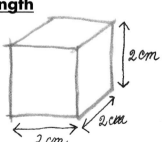

Scientific Notation

Scientific notation is a way of writing a very large or very small number as the product of two factors. The first factor is a number between **0** and **10**. The second factor is a power of **10** written with an exponent.

Question: **What is the distance between the Sun and Earth?**

standard notation
$$\begin{cases} 93 \text{ million miles} \\ 93{,}000{,}000 \text{ miles} \\ 93 \times 1{,}000{,}000 \text{ miles} \\ 9.3 \times 10{,}000{,}000 \text{ miles} \end{cases}$$

Sun ←———————————————————→ **Earth**

scientific notation 9.3×10^{7} miles

| First factor is a number between 0 and 10. | Second factor is a power of 10. |

In 9.3×10^{7}, the exponent is **7**. There are **7** digits after the **9** in **93,000,000**.

Writing a number in scientific notation does not change its value. We use scientific notation because it makes adding, subtracting, multiplying, and dividing very large or very small numbers easier.

Find out more about *exponents* on page 35.

Similar Figures

Geometric figures are **similar** if they have the same shape but not necessarily the same size. Here are some things that suggest the idea of similarity.

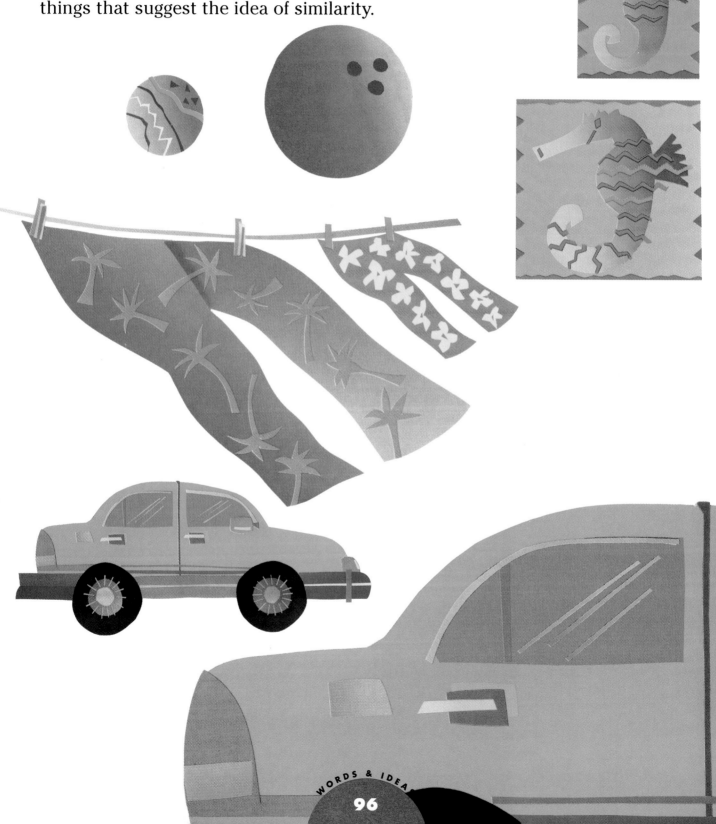

The symbol ~ means *is similar to.*

$\triangle$ **ABC** ~ $\triangle$ **DEF**.
We say that triangle **ABC** is similar to triangle **DEF**. This means that the matching angles are congruent and that the matching sides are proportional.

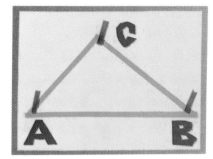

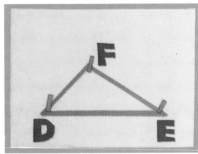

$\angle A = \angle D$

$\angle B = \angle E$

$\angle C = \angle F$

$\angle A$ is congruent to $\angle D$.

$\angle B$ is congruent to $\angle E$.

$\angle C$ is congruent to $\angle F$.

$$\frac{AB}{DE} = \frac{BC}{EF} = \frac{CA}{FD}$$

Matching sides are proportional.

Similar figures that are flipped and turned are still similar.

When figures have the same shape and the same size they are called **congruent figures**.

Find out more about *congruent figures* on pages 18–19.

Statistics

We can use **statistics** to describe **data**. Data are collected for many reasons. We may want to know how many people live in a country, what ice cream flavor our class likes most, or how quickly animals move.

Data can be collected by taking measurements, conducting surveys, or interviewing. Once data are collected, we can use graphs for display and tables for organization.

We can use the **mean**, **median**, **mode**, and **range** to analyze or describe a set of collected data. Here are some ways to describe the number of laps students walked in their school walk-a-thon.

Student	Number of Laps Each Student Walked
Stuart	12
Mei	14
Carlos	16
Ryan	16
Keisha	18
Judy	20
Miguel	23

The mean or average number of laps is **17**.

The median number of laps is **16**.

The mode for this data set is **16**.

The range between the highest number and the lowest number of laps is **11**.

Find out more about *statistics* on pages 10, 55, 58, and 59.

Subtraction

Subtraction is an operation we use to separate or compare groups.

Here is a separating situation.

There are 85 bees altogether.
12 are flying away.
How many are still on the beekeeper?

Here is another kind of subtraction situation.

The hive has 60 bees inside.
There are 48 worker bees.
How many are not worker bees?

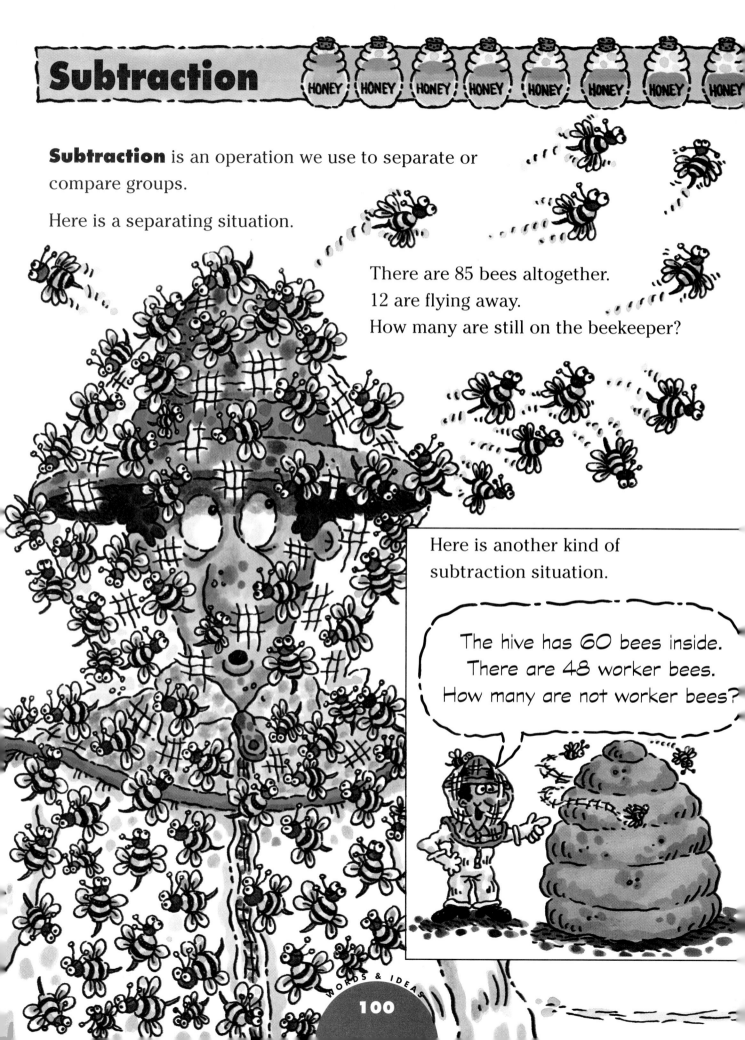

Here is a comparing situation.

There are special names and symbols
we use for subtraction.

subtraction symbol

equal sign

46 − 18 = 28

minuend   subtrahend   difference

There are different ways to subtract.

124 − 68 = ?

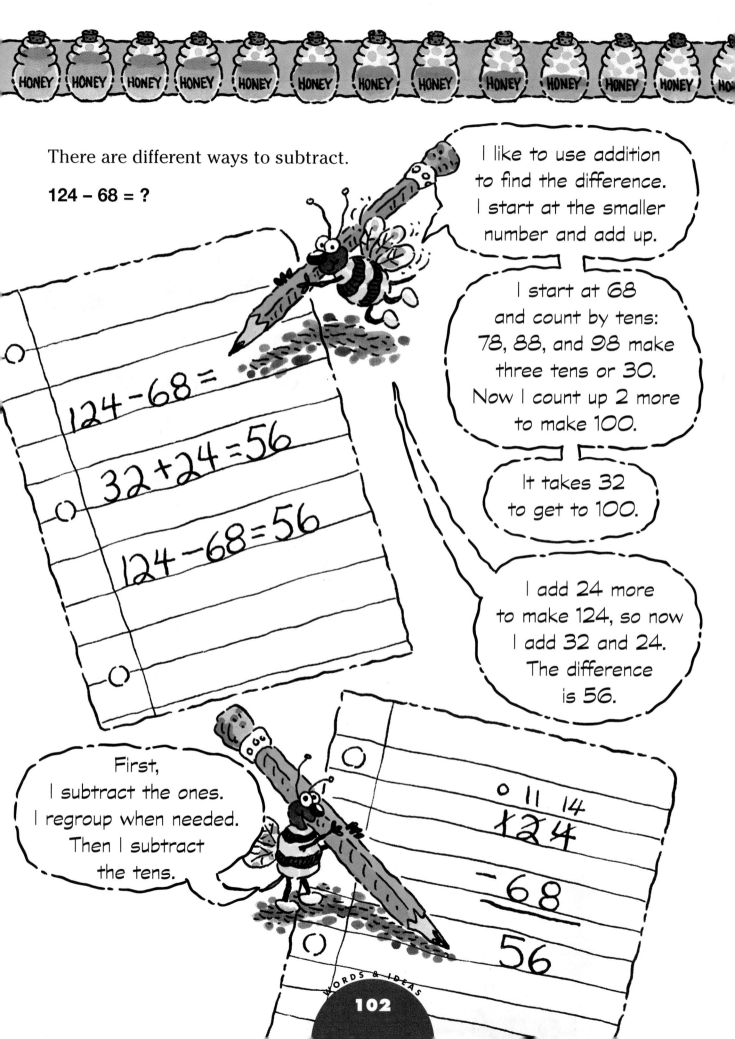

I like to use addition to find the difference. I start at the smaller number and add up.

I start at 68 and count by tens: 78, 88, and 98 make three tens or 30. Now I count up 2 more to make 100.

It takes 32 to get to 100.

I add 24 more to make 124, so now I add 32 and 24. The difference is 56.

First, I subtract the ones. I regroup when needed. Then I subtract the tens.

I'll use my calculator. First I'll estimate. 120 minus 70 is 50, so the difference is about 50. Now I'll push the buttons.

We can use addition to check subtraction.

124 – 68 = 56

Check the answer by adding the difference to the subtrahend:

56 + 68 = 124

Because **56** and **68** make **124**, we know **56** is the correct difference.

Symmetry

A figure or object has **line symmetry** if one or more lines can be drawn to separate it into parts that are the same size and shape. A line that separates a figure or object into identical parts is called a **line of symmetry**. Some figures and objects have only one line of symmetry, while others have two or more lines of symmetry.

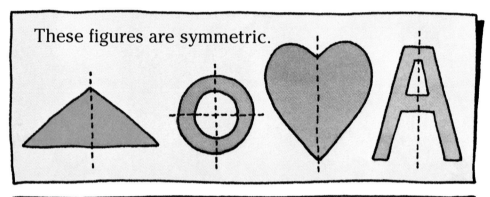

These figures are symmetric.

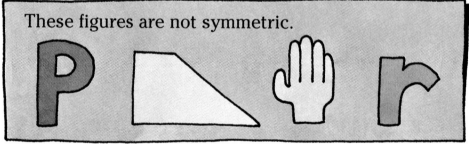

These figures are not symmetric.

An object or figure has **turn** or **rotational symmetry** if its appearance is unchanged after it is turned less than **360°**. Block letters, such as **H**, **I**, and **O**, are examples of figures with both line symmetry and turn symmetry at **180°**.

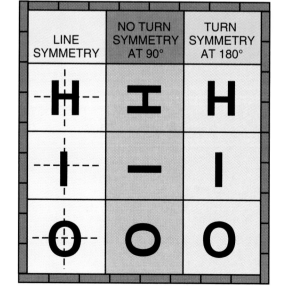

LINE SYMMETRY	NO TURN SYMMETRY AT 90°	TURN SYMMETRY AT 180°
H	H	H
I	—	I
O	O	O

A **tessellation** is an arrangement of closed shapes that completely covers a plane (flat surface) without overlapping and without leaving gaps.

A honeycomb built by bees is an example of a simple tessellation found in nature that is made of regular hexagons. Floor tiles and brick fireplaces are examples of tessellating patterns made by humans.

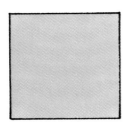

To make a tessellation, start with a square or other regular quadrilateral cut out of heavy paper.

Cut an irregular shape from one side of the quadrilateral, slide it to the opposite side, and attach it with tape.

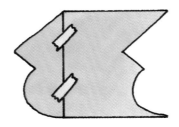

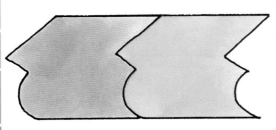

Trace the new figure, slide the cut-out shape vertically or horizontally, and then trace again. Continue tracing until you have filled the plane.

tessellation

Another tessellation can be made by cutting a quadrilateral out of heavy paper, rotating the figure around the midpoint of any side, and tracing. Continue rotating and tracing to form the tessellation.

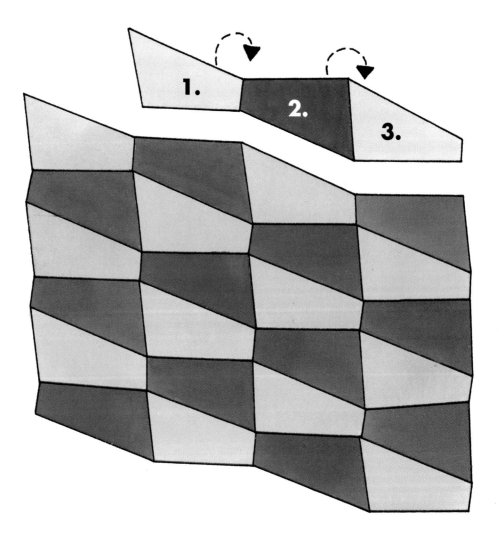

Find out more about *motion geometry* on page 62.

We can measure **time** in seconds, hours, days, weeks, months, or years.

The ancient Babylonians divided each hour in a day into **60** equal parts. Later the ancient Romans used the same system and called each division *par minuta* (a minute). They also divided each minute into **60** equal parts and called each division *par seconda* (a second). That is why today we have **60** minutes in an hour and **60** seconds in a minute.

To describe the hours in a day, we use **standard time**. Using standard time means we divide the day into two parts, with twelve hours in each part.

The twelve hours from midnight to noon are labeled **a.m.**, which is Latin for *ante meridiem*, meaning before midday. The twelve hours from noon to midnight are labeled **p.m.**, which is Latin for *post meridiem*, meaning after midday.

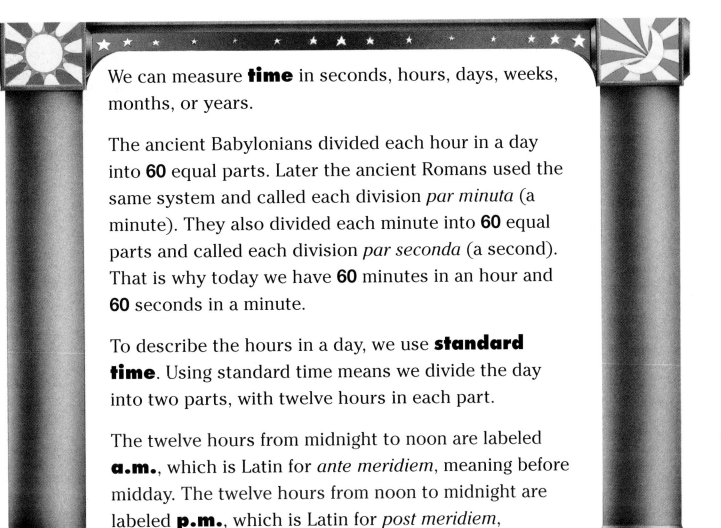

12:00 AM	7:15 AM	12:00 PM	3:45 PM	8:05 PM
midnight	**breakfast**	**noon**	**play**	**homework**

Sometimes standard time can be confusing. Six o'clock could mean six in the morning or evening. To avoid confusion we can use **military time**, where the hours beginning at midnight are numbered 1 through 24.

When we use military time we describe the time in a special way. If it were 7:00 a.m. we would not call it *seven o'clock*, but *0700*.

Standard Time	Military Time
12:00 a.m. (midnight)	0000 hours
9:00 a.m.	0900 hours
12:00 p.m. (noon)	1200 hours
9:00 p.m.	2100 hours

My plane leaves at 1400 hours.

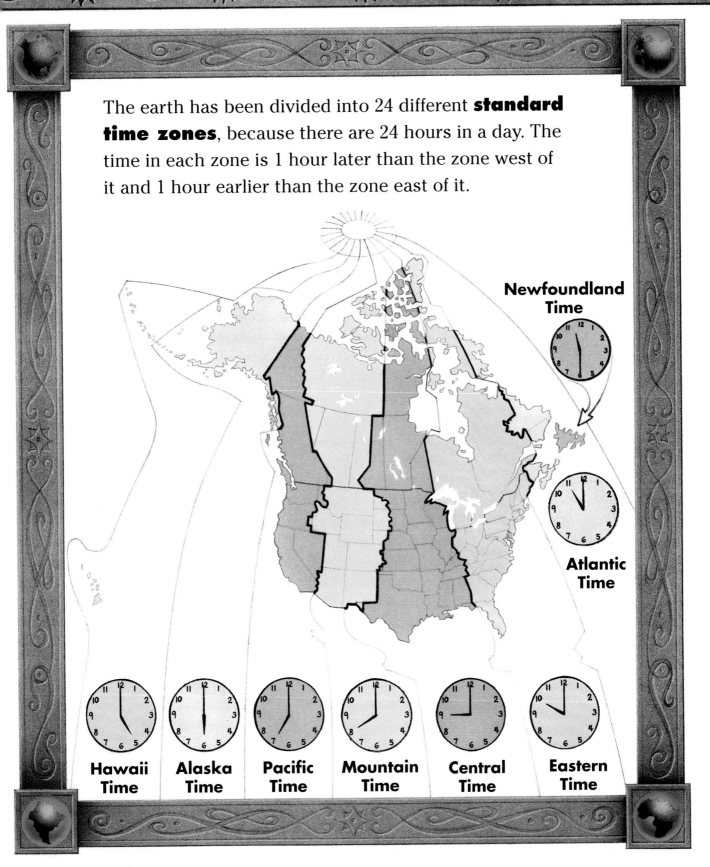

The earth has been divided into 24 different **standard time zones**, because there are 24 hours in a day. The time in each zone is 1 hour later than the zone west of it and 1 hour earlier than the zone east of it.

Newfoundland Time

Atlantic Time

Hawaii Time

Alaska Time

Pacific Time

Mountain Time

Central Time

Eastern Time

Find out more about *time equivalencies* on pages 124–125.

Triangles

A **triangle** is a polygon with three sides. Triangles are classified by their angles and the lengths of their sides.

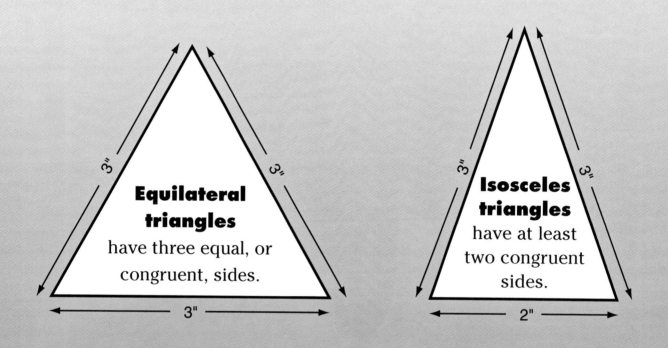

Equilateral triangles have three equal, or congruent, sides.

3"   3"   3"

Isosceles triangles have at least two congruent sides.

3"   3"   2"

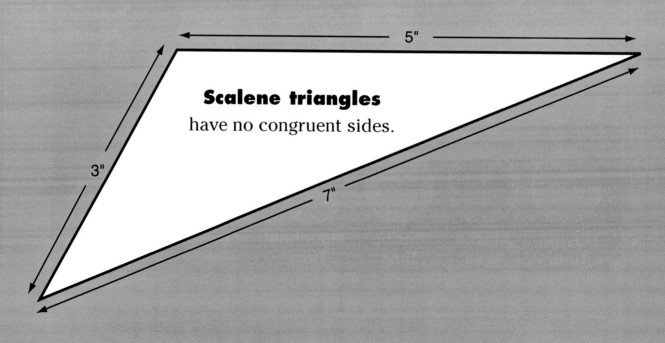

Scalene triangles have no congruent sides.

5"   3"   7"

triangles

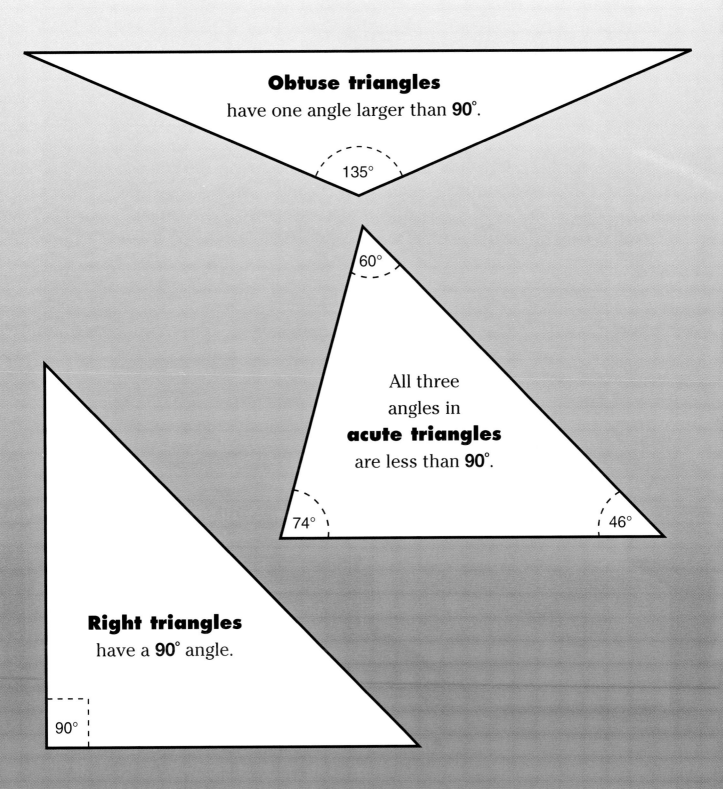

Obtuse triangles
have one angle larger than **90°**.

135°

60°

All three
angles in
acute triangles
are less than **90°**.

74°

46°

Right triangles
have a **90°** angle.

90°

Find out more about *angles* on pages 6–7.

Volume

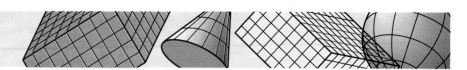

Volume is a measure of space occupied by a three-dimensional object. We can measure volume in cubic units such as cubic inches or cubic centimeters.

1 cubic inch (in.³)

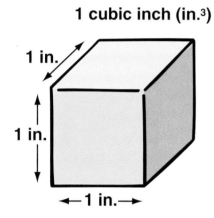

1 in.

1 in.

←1 in.→

1 cubic centimeter (cm³)

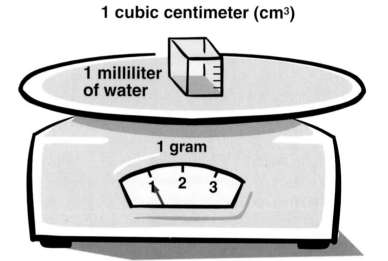

1 milliliter of water

1 gram

One cubic centimeter holds one milliliter of water which weighs one gram!

400 cubic inches (in.³)

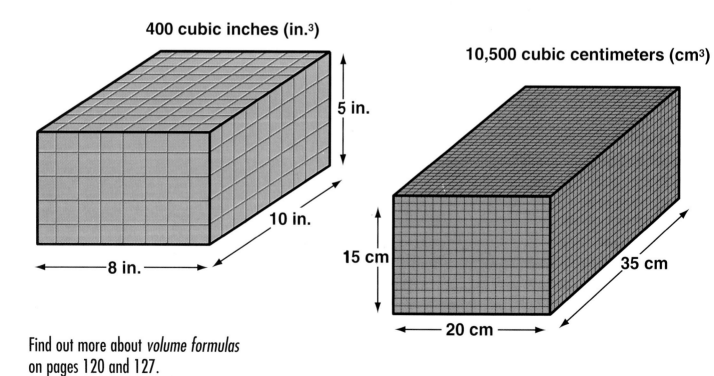

5 in.

10 in.

8 in.

10,500 cubic centimeters (cm³)

15 cm

35 cm

20 cm

Find out more about *volume formulas* on pages 120 and 127.

Weight

Weight is the measure of the force that gravity exerts on an object.

Sometimes the terms weight and mass are used interchangeably but they are not the same. (See definition of *mass*, page 54.)

Here are common units of measure for weight in the customary and metric systems.

Customary Measures

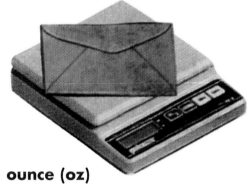

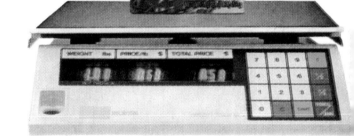

pound (lb)
Brown sugar is sold in one pound boxes.

ounce (oz)
A letter usually weighs less than an ounce.

ton (T)
A small truck weighs about one ton.

weight

Metric Measures

gram (g)
A paperclip weighs about one gram.

kilogram (kg)
A baseball bat weighs about one kilogram.

metric ton (t)
A female elephant seal
weighs about one metric ton.

Find out more about *customary* and
metric measurement on page 128.

Formulas and Equivalencies

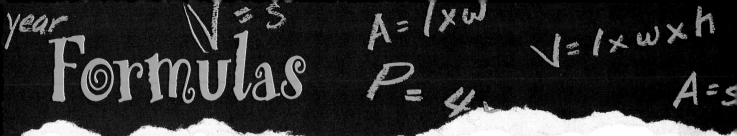

Formulas

Area

Square

Area = $s \times s$

$A = s \times s$

or

$A = s^2$

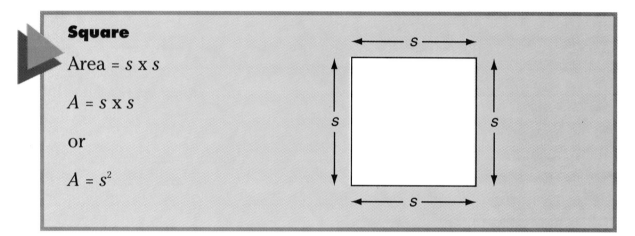

Rectangle

Area = length x width

$A = l \times w$

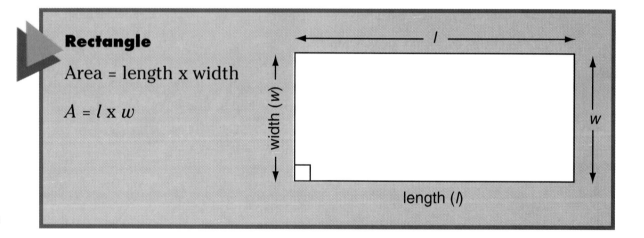

Triangle

Area = $\frac{1}{2}$ x base x height

$A = \frac{1}{2} \times b \times h$

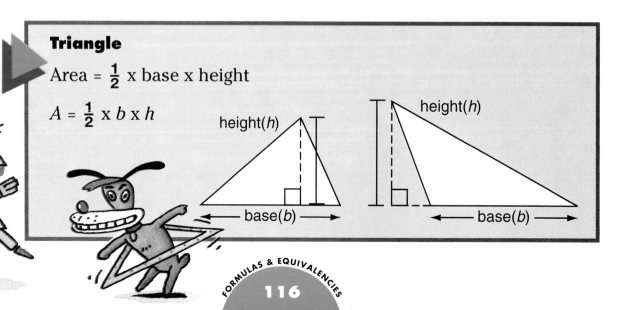

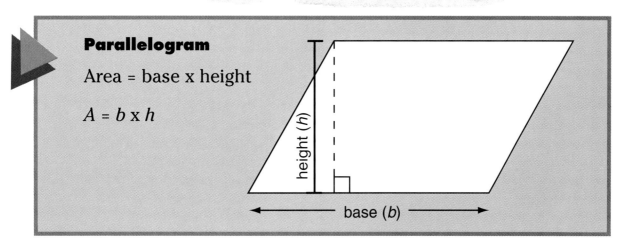

Parallelogram

Area = base x height

$A = b \times h$

Circle

Area = π x radius x radius

$A = \pi \times r \times r$

or

$A = \pi \times r^2$

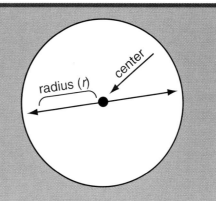

radius (r)   center

Trapezoid

Area = $\frac{1}{2}$ x (base$_1$ + base$_2$) x height

$A = \frac{1}{2} \times (b_1 + b_2) \times h$

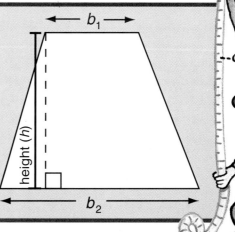

b_1

height (h)

b_2

Perimeter and Circumference

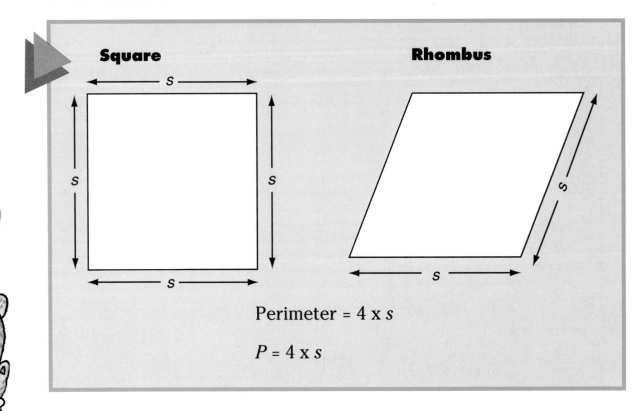

Square

Rhombus

Perimeter = 4 x s

$P = 4 \times s$

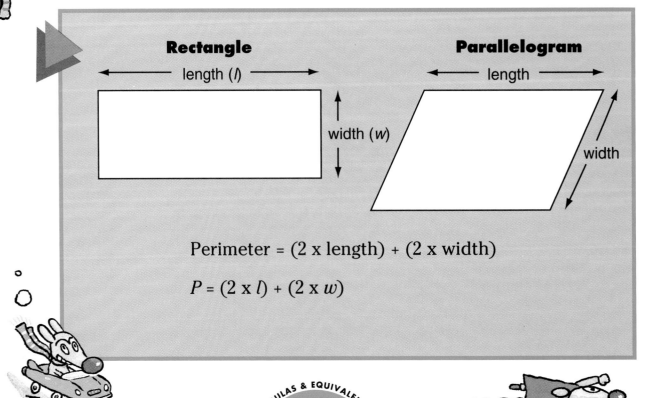

Rectangle

length (l)

width (w)

Parallelogram

length

width

Perimeter = (2 x length) + (2 x width)

$P = (2 \times l) + (2 \times w)$

$P = 4 \times s$ $C = 2 \times \pi \times r$ 1 ft. = 12 in.

1 yd. = 3 ft. $V = s^3$ year $V =$

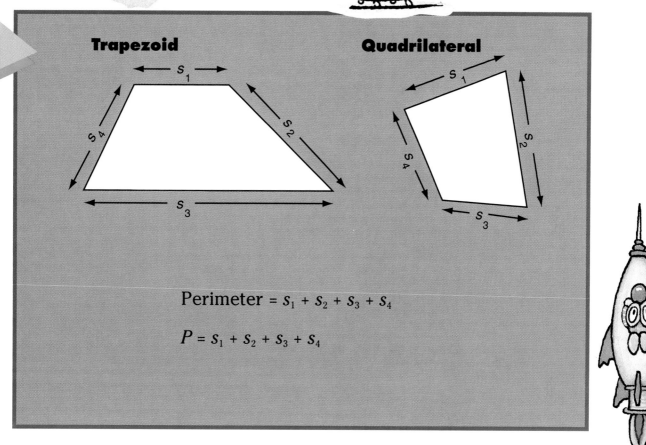

Trapezoid

Quadrilateral

Perimeter = $s_1 + s_2 + s_3 + s_4$

$P = s_1 + s_2 + s_3 + s_4$

Circle

Circumference = π x diameter

$C = \pi \times d$

and

Circumference = 2 x π x radius

$C = 2 \times \pi \times r$

circumference (c)

center

radius (r)

diameter (d)

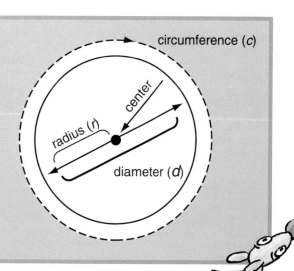

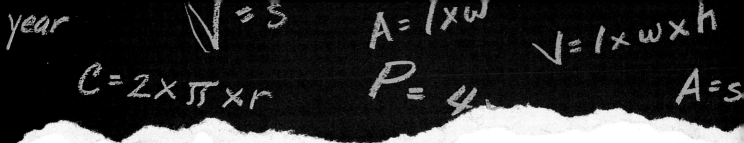

Volume

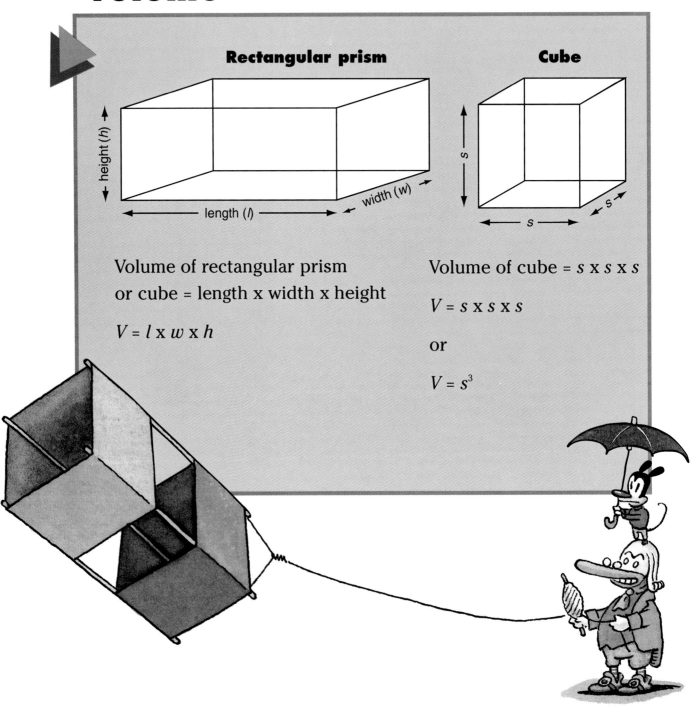

Rectangular prism

height (h)

length (l)

width (w)

Cube

s

s

s

Volume of rectangular prism
or cube = length x width x height

$V = l \times w \times h$

Volume of cube = $s \times s \times s$

$V = s \times s \times s$

or

$V = s^3$

Equivalencies

Capacity

Customary System

1 fluid ounce (fl. oz) = 2 tablespoons (tbsp)
1 cup (c) = 8 fluid ounces (fl. oz)
1 pint (pt) = 16 fluid ounces (fl. oz)
1 pint (pt) = 2 cups (c)
1 quart (qt) = 4 cups (c)
1 quart (qt) = 2 pints (pt)
1 gallon (gal) = 16 cups (c)
1 gallon (gal) = 8 pints (pt)
1 gallon (gal) = 4 quarts (qt)

Metric System

1 liter (L) = 1,000 milliliters (mL)

A **half pint** or **1 cup** or **8 ounces**

A **half gallon** or **two quarts** of milk

A **gallon** of milk

About **350 milliliters**

A **liter**

Length

CUSTOMARY SYSTEM

1 foot (ft) = 12 inches (in.)
1 yard (yd) = 36 inches (in.) = 3 feet (ft)
1 mile (mi) = 5,280 feet (ft) = 1,760 yards (yd)

METRIC SYSTEM

1 centimeter (cm) = 10 millimeters (mm)
1 decimeter (dm) = 10 centimeters (cm) = 100 millimeters (mm)
1 meter (m) = 10 decimeters (dm) = 100 centimeters (cm) = 1,000 millimeters (mm)
1 kilometer (km) = 1,000 meters (m)

Your little finger is about a **centimeter** wide.

The length of your thumb from the knuckle to the tip is about an **inch**.

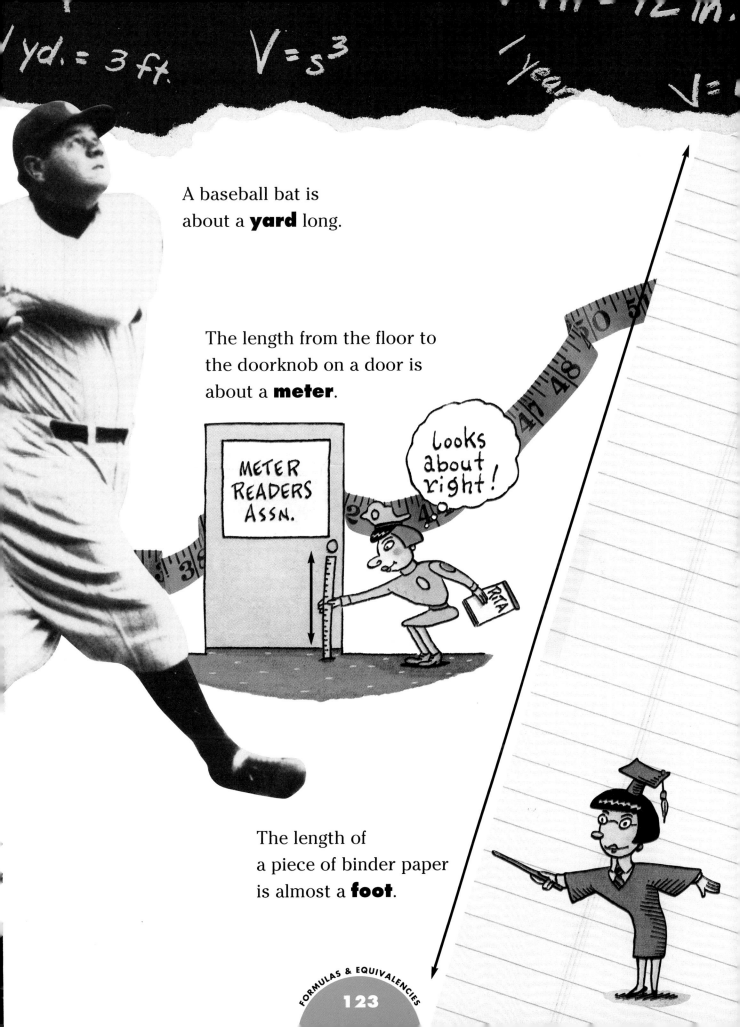

A baseball bat is about a **yard** long.

The length from the floor to the doorknob on a door is about a **meter**.

The length of a piece of binder paper is almost a **foot**.

Time

1 minute (min) = 60 seconds (s)

1 hour (h) = 60 minutes (min)

1 day (d) = 24 hours (h)

1 week (w) = 7 days (d)

1 month (mo) = about 4 weeks

1 year (yr) = 365 days

1 leap year = 366 days

1 year = 52 weeks

1 year = 12 months

1 decade = 10 years

1 century = 100 years

UH-OH, TiME'S UP!

Temperature

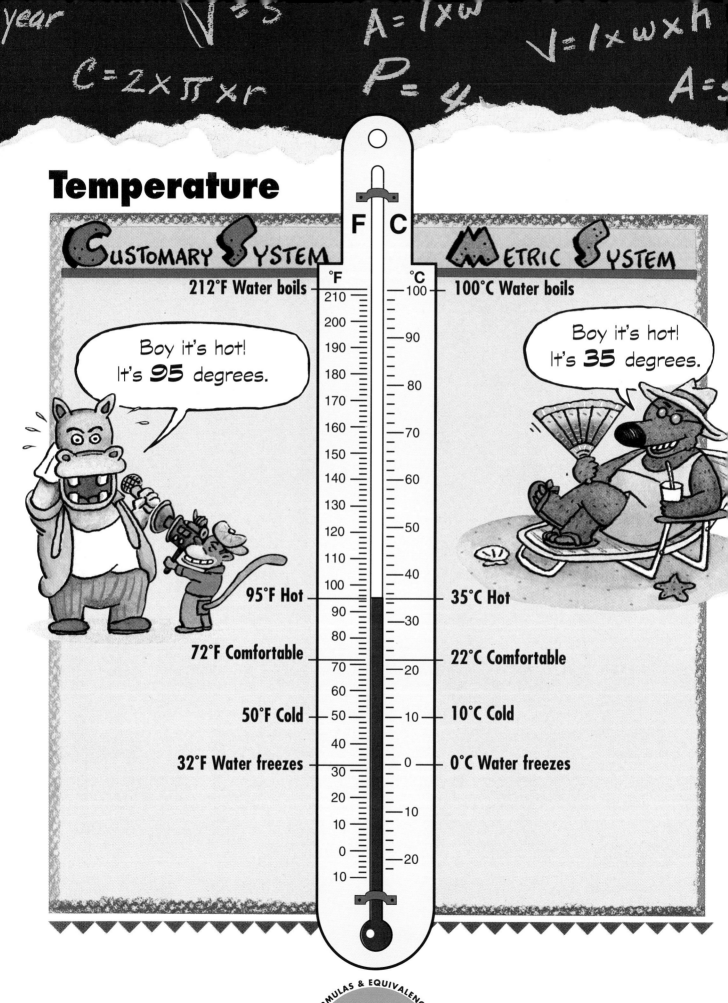

Volume

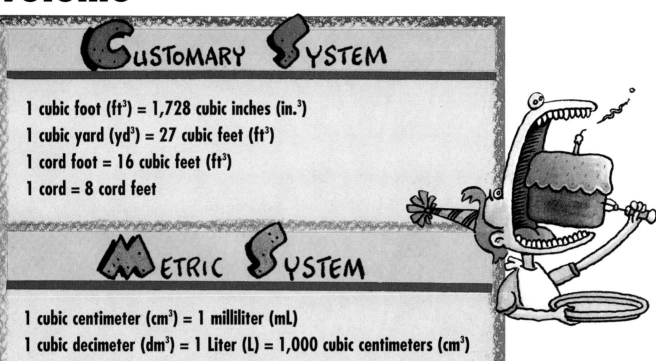

CUSTOMARY SYSTEM

1 cubic foot (ft³) = 1,728 cubic inches (in.³)
1 cubic yard (yd³) = 27 cubic feet (ft³)
1 cord foot = 16 cubic feet (ft³)
1 cord = 8 cord feet

METRIC SYSTEM

1 cubic centimeter (cm³) = 1 milliliter (mL)
1 cubic decimeter (dm³) = 1 Liter (L) = 1,000 cubic centimeters (cm³)

One **cubic foot**

1,000 **cubic centimeters**

Weight/Mass

A telephone weighs about **1 kilogram**.

Customary System

1 pound (lb) = 16 ounces (oz)
1 ton (T) = 2,000 pounds (lb)

Metric System

1 gram (g) = 1,000 milligrams (mg)
1 kilogram (kg) = 1,000 grams (g)
1 metric ton (t) = 1,000 kilograms (kg)

A spoon weighs about **1 ounce**.

A whale weighs about **1 ton**.

A paper clip weighs about **1 gram**.

A soccer ball weighs about **1 pound**.

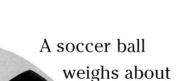

Technology

Calculators

Identifying the Keys

▶ ▶ ▶ ▶ ▶ ▶ ▶ ▶ ▶ ▶ ▶ ▶ ▶ ▶ ▶ ▶ ▶ ▶ ▶ ▶

Clearing

ON/AC — clears memory, the display, and the operation

Backspace — clears the last digit entered

CE/C — clears the display, the operation, the last entry, error conditions, and constants

Fractions

F⮂D — changes a fraction to a decimal number

/ — fraction symbol

Unit — used after the whole number in a mixed number

Simp — simplifies a fraction

Ab/c — changes an improper fraction into a mixed number

x⮂y — identifies the factor used to simplify a fraction

Exponents

10ⁿ — calculates powers of 10

1/x — gives a reciprocal of a whole number or a fraction

yˣ — calculates powers and roots

x² — squares a number

√ — calculates square root

Memory

Cons — stores an operation and a number

x⮂M — exchanges the displayed value with a value in the memory

M− — subtracts the displayed value from the memory

M+ — adds the displayed value to the memory

MR — displays the value stored in the memory

Decimals and Percent

Fix	sets the number of decimal places
·	decimal point
%	changes a percentage into a decimal

Operations

(	opens parentheses
)	closes parentheses
INT÷	gives a division quotient with remainders
÷	divides
×	multiplies
−	subtracts
+	adds
+↺−	displays positive and negative integers
=	equals or repeats an operation

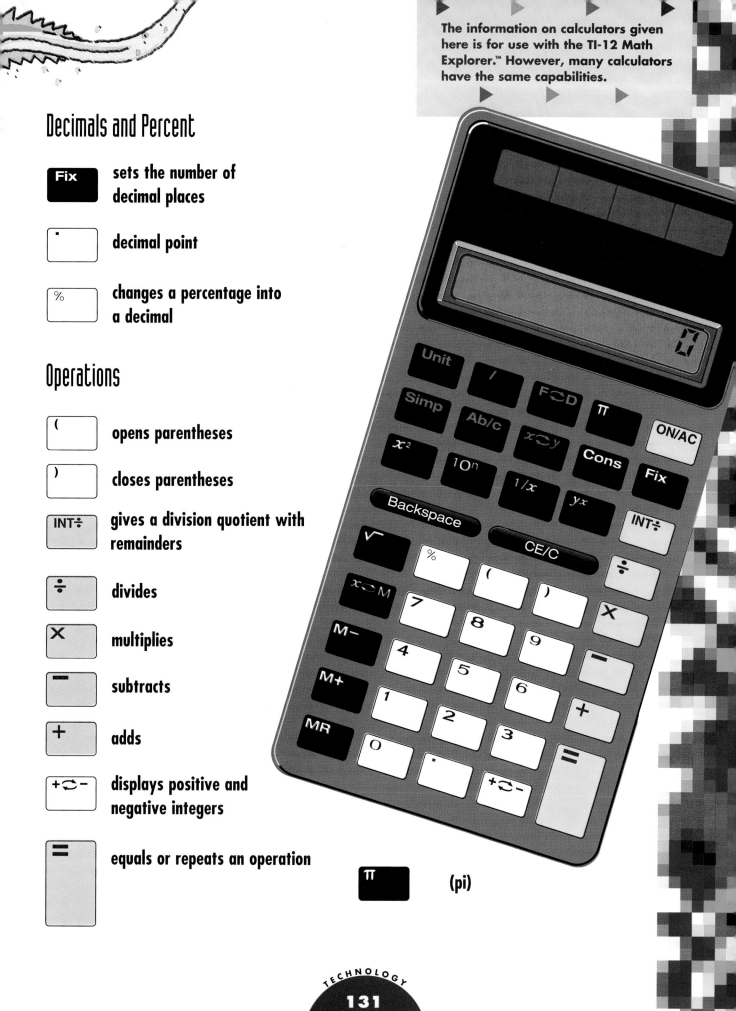

| π | (pi) |

Operations

▶ ▶ ▶ ▶ ▶ ▶ ▶ ▶ ▶ ▶ ▶ ▶ ▶

Here are some ways we can use the calculator to **add**, **subtract**, **multiply**, or **divide**. Enter the numbers and operations just the way you say the problem.

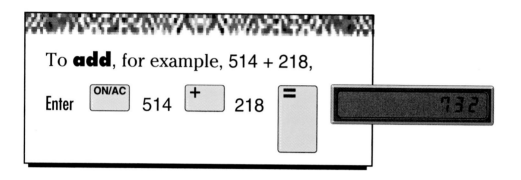

To **add**, for example, 514 + 218,

Enter [ON/AC] 514 [+] 218 [=]   732

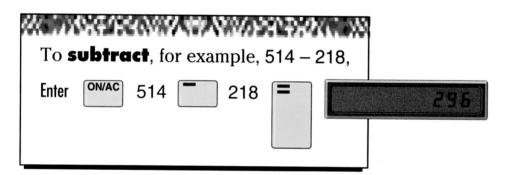

To **subtract**, for example, 514 – 218,

Enter [ON/AC] 514 [–] 218 [=]   296

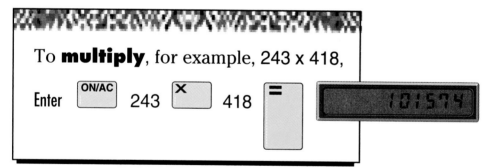

To **multiply**, for example, 243 x 418,

Enter [ON/AC] 243 [×] 418 [=]   101574

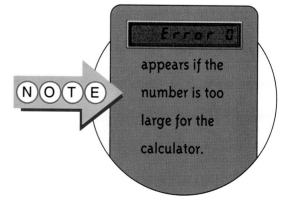

N O T E ▶ *Error 0* appears if the number is too large for the calculator.

The calculator has two **division** keys.

The [÷] displays the remainder as a decimal fraction.

The [INT÷] displays the remainder as a whole number.

To **divide**, for example, 254 ÷ 45,

Enter [ON/AC] 254 [÷] 45 [=]   `5.6444444`

Here is one way you could write the answer. 5.6$\overline{4}$

Here is another way to **divide**,

Enter [ON/AC] 254 [INT÷] 45 [=]   `5      29`
                                   Q   R

Here is one way you could write the answer. 5R29

`Error 5` appears if the numbers used with [INT÷] are not positive whole numbers.

N O T E

133

Order of Operations

▶▶▶▶▶▶▶▶▶▶▶▶▶▶▶▶▶▶▶▶▶▶

The Math Explorer™ calculator follows the **order of operations**. You can enter the problem just as it is written.

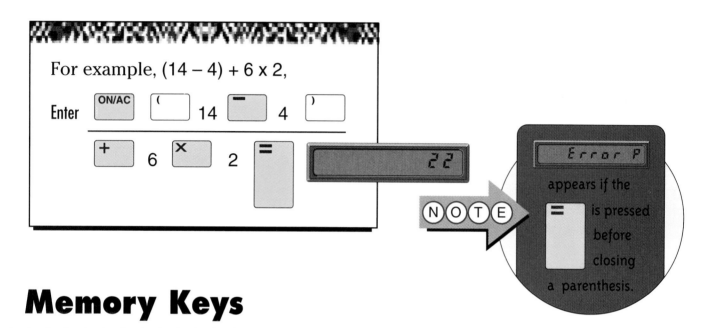

For example, (14 − 4) + 6 x 2,

Enter | ON/AC | (| 14 | ▬ | 4 |) |

| + | 6 | X | 2 | = |

Display: 22

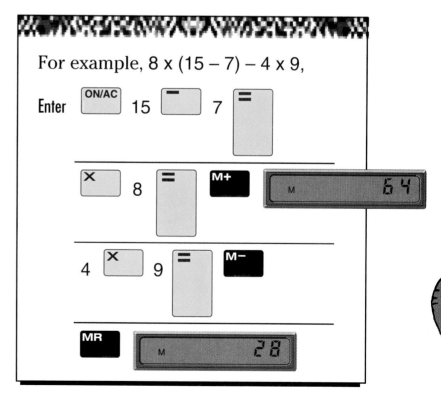

NOTE: Error P appears if the = is pressed before closing a parenthesis.

Memory Keys

▶▶▶▶▶▶▶▶▶▶▶▶▶▶▶

The **memory keys** on the calculator allow you to store the result of one calculation while you do another calculation.

You can use the memory keys to solve a problem with many operations.

For example, 8 x (15 − 7) − 4 x 9,

Enter | ON/AC | 15 | ▬ | 7 | = |

| X | 8 | = | M+ |

Display: M 64

| 4 | X | 9 | = | M− |

| MR |

Display: M 28

To Repeat an Operation

▶▶▶▶▶▶▶▶▶▶▶▶▶▶▶▶▶▶▶▶▶▶▶▶▶▶▶▶▶▶

Many calculators have a built-in constant that allows you to repeat an operation without having to press more than one key. The **constant** or ⬛**Cons** allows you to add, subtract, multiply, or divide by the same number repeatedly. So does the **equals** key.

Here is one way to **repeat addition**.

Here is one way to **repeat division**.

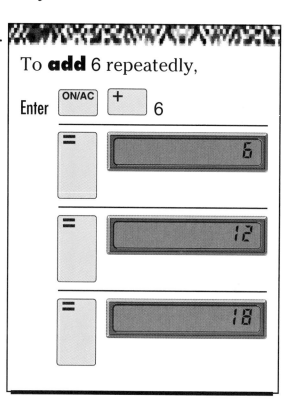

To **add** 6 repeatedly,

Enter ⬜ON/AC ⬜+ 6

= | 6

= | 12

= | 18

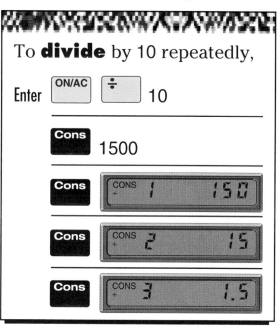

To **divide** by 10 repeatedly,

Enter ⬜ON/AC ⬜÷ 10

⬛Cons 1500

⬛Cons | CONS ÷ 1 150

⬛Cons | CONS ÷ 2 15

⬛Cons | CONS ÷ 3 1.5

Here are some ways to **repeat multiplication**.

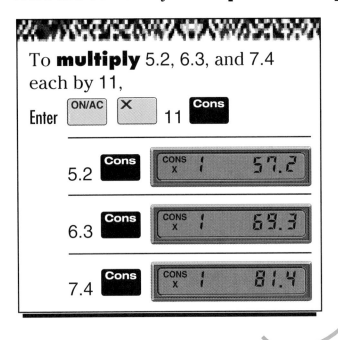

To **multiply** 5.2, 6.3, and 7.4 each by 11,

Enter [ON/AC] [X] 11 [Cons]

5.2 [Cons] CONS X 1   57.2

6.3 [Cons] CONS X 1   69.3

7.4 [Cons] CONS X 1   81.4

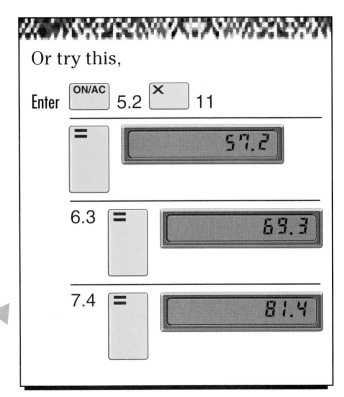

Or try this,

Enter [ON/AC] 5.2 [X] 11

[=]   57.2

6.3 [=]   69.3

7.4 [=]   81.4

We can also use the constant key to identify multiples of a number.

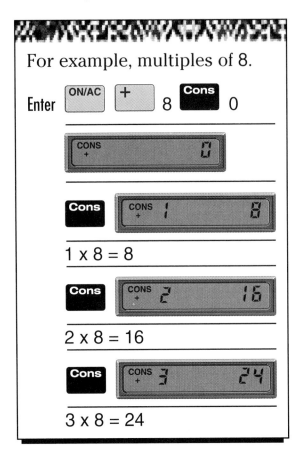

For example, multiples of 8.

Enter [ON/AC] [+] 8 [Cons] 0

CONS +   0

[Cons] CONS + 1   8

1 x 8 = 8

[Cons] CONS + 2   16

2 x 8 = 16

[Cons] CONS + 3   24

3 x 8 = 24

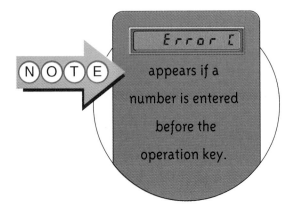

N O T E

Error C

appears if a number is entered before the operation key.

Decimals

▶ ▶ ▶ ▶ ▶ ▶ ▶ ▶ ▶ ▶ ▶ ▶ ▶

When you enter decimal numbers on your calculator, remember to enter [·].

Notice that the calculator places a zero in front of the decimal point if you do not enter a whole number.

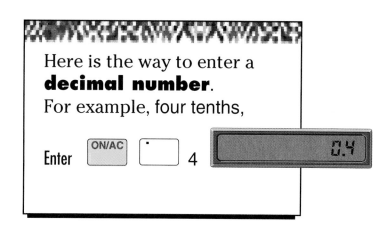

Here is the way to enter a **decimal number**.
For example, four tenths,

Enter [ON/AC] [·] 4   0.4

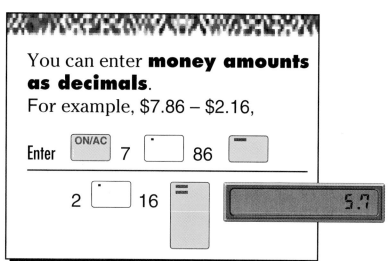

You can enter **money amounts as decimals**.
For example, $7.86 – $2.16,

Enter [ON/AC] 7 [·] 86 [ ]

2 [·] 16 [ ]   5.7

Here is one way you could write the answer. $5.70

Working with Fractions

Changing from Fractions to Decimals

▶▶▶▶▶▶▶▶▶▶▶▶▶▶▶▶▶▶▶▶▶▶▶

To express a **fraction as a decimal** you can use your calculator to divide the numerator by the denominator, or use the 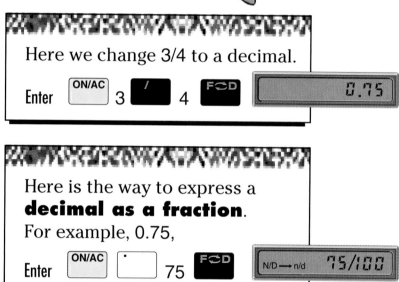.

The ⬛ separates the numerator from the denominator.

The N/D ➔ n/d in the display means that the fraction is not in **simplest form**.

Here we change 3/4 to a decimal.

Enter `ON/AC` 3 `/` 4 `F⇄D`   `0.75`

Here is the way to express a **decimal as a fraction**. For example, 0.75,

Enter `ON/AC` `·` 75 `F⇄D`   `N/D—n/d  75/100`

Simplifying Fractions

▶▶▶▶▶▶▶▶▶▶▶▶▶▶▶▶▶▶▶▶▶▶▶

One way you can **simplify fractions** is to enter `Simp` `=` until N/D ➔ n/d disappears from the display.

Use `x⇄y` to show the **factor** used in simplifying. Five is a factor of **15** and **20**.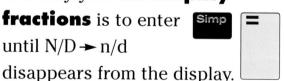

To change back to a fraction press `x⇄y` again.

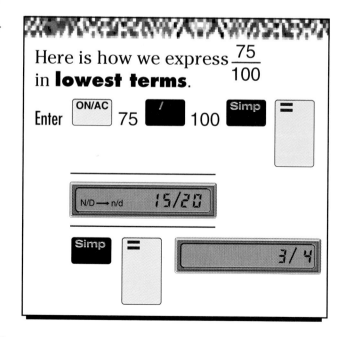

Here is how we express $\frac{75}{100}$ in **lowest terms**.

Enter `ON/AC` 75 `/` 100 `Simp` `=`

`N/D—n/d  15/20`

`Simp` `=`   `3/4`

Another way to simplify a fraction is by using a factor you choose.

If you choose an incorrect factor the original fraction appears again on the display.

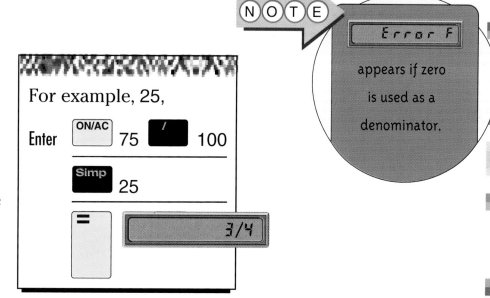

For example, 25,

Enter [ON/AC] 75 [/] 100

[Simp] 25

[=]   3/4

NOTE

Error F

appears if zero is used as a denominator.

Add, Subtract, Multiply, or Divide Fractions

▸ ▸

To add, subtract, multiply, or divide fractions on the calculator, enter the problems just the way they are written. In addition and subtraction of fractions, the calculator shows the answer with the lowest common denominator.

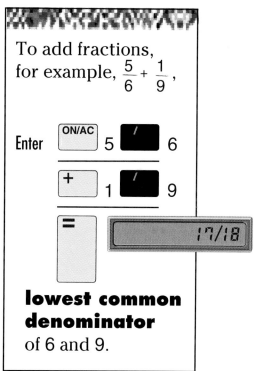

To add fractions, for example, $\frac{5}{6} + \frac{1}{9}$,

Enter [ON/AC] 5 [/] 6

[+] 1 [/] 9

[=]   17/18

lowest common denominator of 6 and 9.

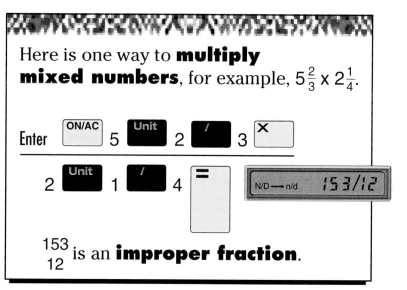

Here is one way to **multiply mixed numbers**, for example, $5\frac{2}{3} \times 2\frac{1}{4}$.

Enter [ON/AC] 5 [Unit] 2 [/] 3 [×]

2 [Unit] 1 [/] 4 [=]   N/D → n/d   153/12

$\frac{153}{12}$ is an **improper fraction**.

We can also use the calculator to add, subtract, multiply, or divide **mixed numbers**. The [Unit] shows the whole number or unit part of a mixed number.

Changing Improper Fractions to Mixed Numbers

▶ ▶

Here is the way to change an improper fraction.

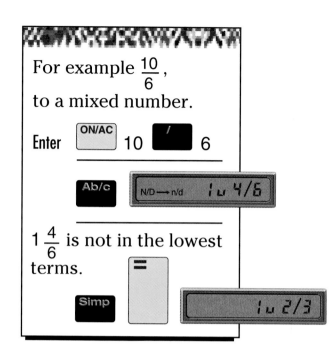

For example $\frac{10}{6}$, to a mixed number.

Enter [ON/AC] 10 [/] 6

[Ab/c] [N/D⟶n/d] $1 \cup 4/6$

$1\frac{4}{6}$ is not in the lowest terms.

[=]

[Simp] $1 \cup 2/3$

Changing Percents to Decimals and Fractions

▶ ▶ ▶ ▶ ▶ ▶ ▶ ▶ ▶ ▶ ▶ ▶ ▶ ▶ ▶ ▶ ▶ ▶ ▶

The [%] changes the **number** in the display to a decimal by dividing it by **100**.

Here is a way to find the **decimal for a percent**.

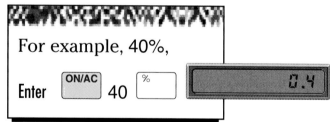

For example, 40%,

Enter [ON/AC] 40 [%] 0.4

Here is a way to find the **fraction** for a percent.

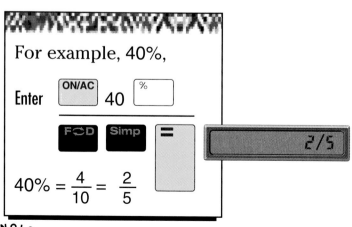

For example, 40%,

Enter [ON/AC] 40 [%]

[F⟷D] [Simp] [=] $2/5$

$40\% = \frac{4}{10} = \frac{2}{5}$

Computing with Integers

▸▸▸▸▸▸▸▸▸▸▸▸▸▸▸▸▸▸▸▸▸▸▸▸

The ⌈+⟳−⌉ changes the sign of the number in the display. Here is a way to change the sign of a number.

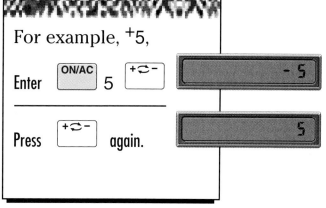

For example, $^+5$,

Enter [ON/AC] 5 [+⟳−]   ▢ − 5

Press [+⟳−] again.   ▢ 5

Here is one way to **add integers**.

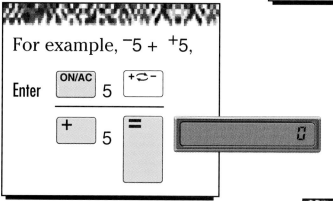

For example, $^-5 + {}^+5$,

Enter [ON/AC] 5 [+⟳−]

[+] 5 [=]   ▢ 0

Here is one way to **subtract integers**.

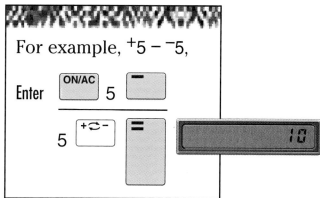

For example, $^+5 - {}^-5$,

Enter [ON/AC] 5 [−]

5 [+⟳−] [=]   ▢ 10

Computers

Computers are electronic devices that can calculate numbers and process information very quickly and accurately. Computers can also sort large amounts of information and solve complicated problems. They help us understand things better by allowing us to make models and test theories.

Using the Computer

First, information is put into the computer. This information is called input or data. Input can be entered into the computer the way that you see here. We can also use video cameras, other computers, satellites, and sensors to input data.

Next the information travels to the internal memory in the central processing unit (CPU).

Then the computer outputs the information. Output can be in the form of numbers, words, graphs, or pictures.

Identifying Parts

Hardware

All computing jobs involve inputting data into the computer, processing and storing it in a special way, and outputting the results. The equipment used to do these jobs is called the hardware.

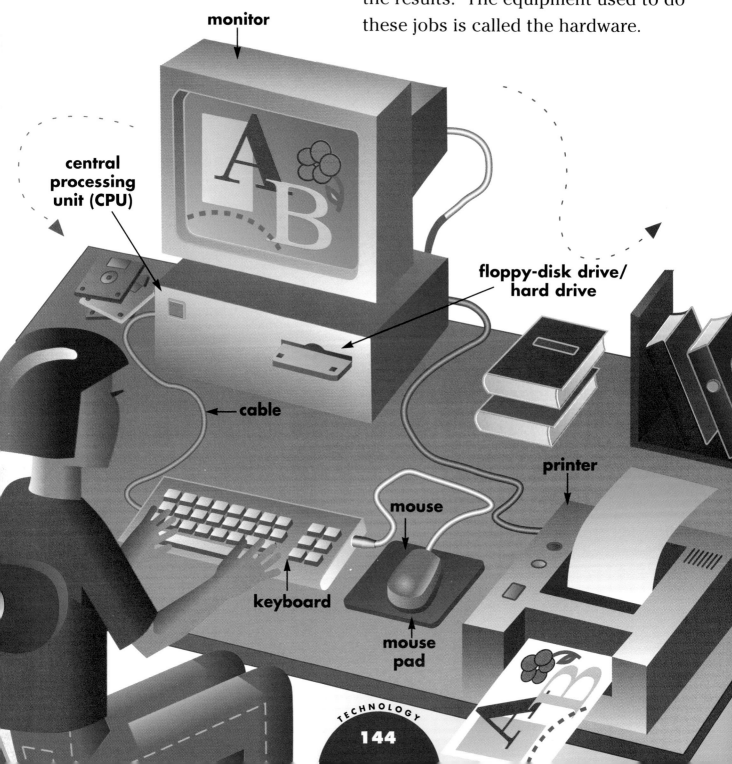

monitor

central processing unit (CPU)

floppy-disk drive/ hard drive

cable

printer

mouse

keyboard

mouse pad

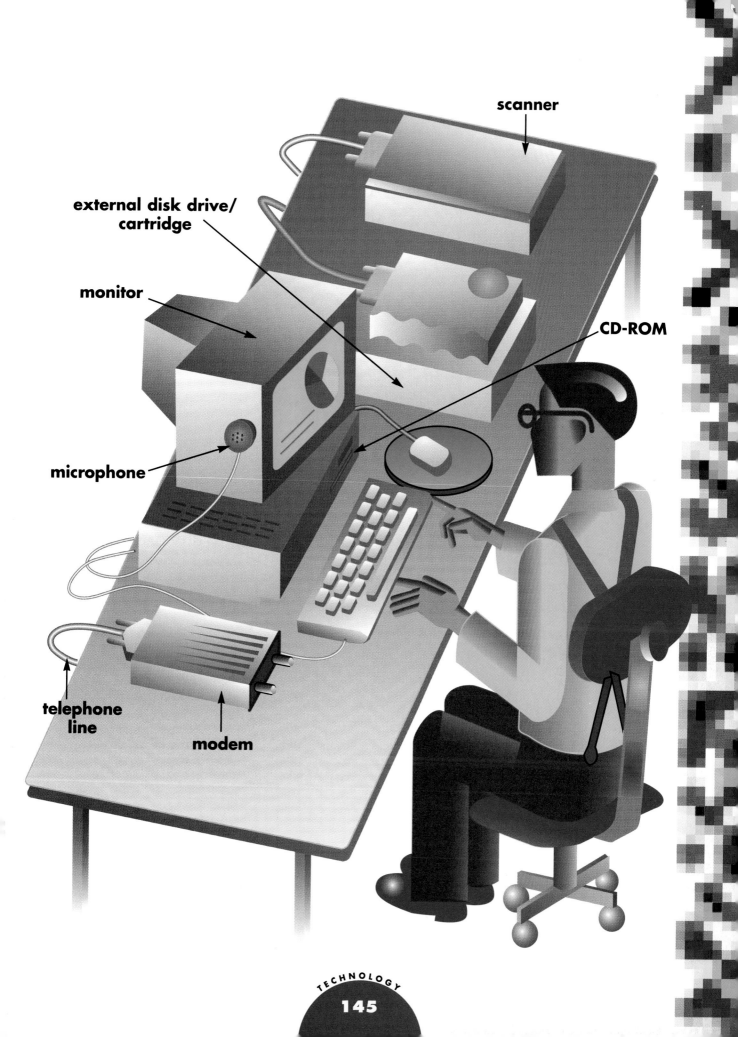

scanner

external disk drive/
cartridge

monitor

CD-ROM

microphone

telephone
line

modem

Software

A **software program** is a list of instructions that is translated into a language that the computer understands. When you play a computer game the instructions and the graphics that drive the game are contained in the software.

Word processing programs allow us to type words into the computer to write, change, and print documents.

Spreadsheet programs have columns and rows. These programs are useful for calculating and making mathematical predictions. They are also helpful for creating tables and drawing graphs.

Databases make it easy for us to work with large amounts of information by helping us store and organize data.

We can use **draw and paint programs** to help us explain our ideas and illustrate information. Some computers can make pictures that look like photographs. Computers with enough memory and the necessary software can show movies, complete with sound.

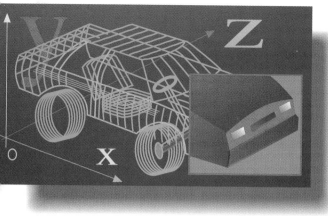

Computer programs that perform **computer-aided design (CAD)** help people, such as book designers, and automobile engineers, experiment first on computers, before they build the final product. These programs save time and increase creativity.

Computers have been used to create simulations of real events. **Simulations** give us an idea of what the actual experience would be like. Some of these simulations are games and others are opportunities to experience or practice things that happen in real life, such as flying an airplane, climbing a mountain, or building a city.

Computer designers have created a computer experience called **virtual reality**.

In some virtual reality programs we use special video goggles and gloves to feel like we really are in a situation. Virtual reality goes beyond simulation by creating an artificial three-dimensional world, where you feel as if you are moving around and touching different objects.

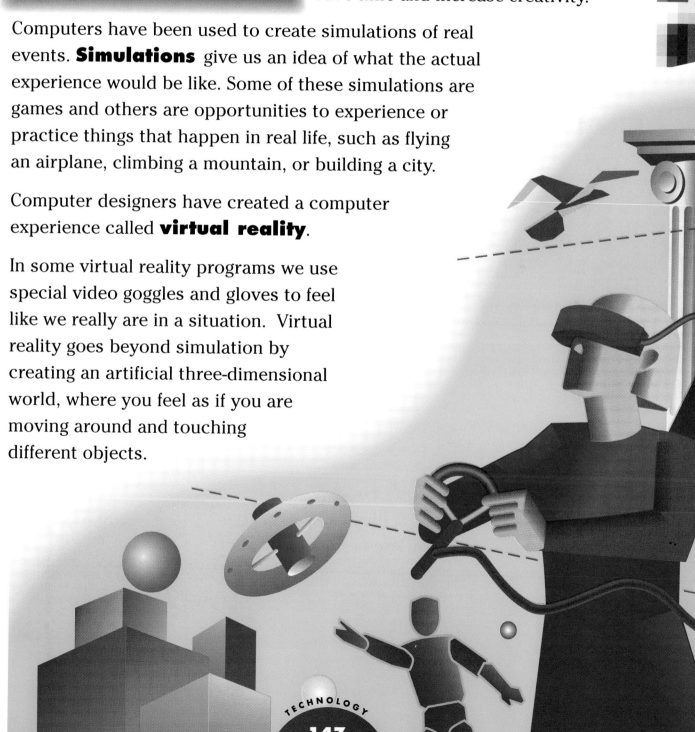

Definitions

Here are some words that
you may hear when people
are talking about computers.

Binary system   Computers count electrically using a binary system. To a computer, a switch that is ON stands for 1, and a switch that is OFF stands for 0 (zero). This is called a binary system because only two digits are used.

Bit   Each 0 or 1 is called a bit. A bit is an abbreviation of the term **bi**nary dig**it**.

Byte   A byte is a group of bits that act as a single unit of information. Usually, eight of these bits of information are grouped together to form one byte. Computer memory is measured in bytes.

Chips   The electronic circuits of a computer are etched into small chips or microchips of silicon. Some chips act as storage, and others act as processors.

A chip is smaller than a postage stamp.

Computer network   Computers can be used to communicate information over long distances. A computer network connects computers that are in different places. We can communicate using computers connected to telephone lines by using electronic mail (e-mail).

CPU   The CPU or central processing unit processes the instructions and information through the computer. It is like a traffic controller, because it directs all the other parts of the computer.

Environment   Environment has a special meaning in the computer world. It refers to the kind of computer, computer language, and operating system that are being used. It is often difficult to change data from one computer environment to another.

Facsimile (Fax)   Fax machines are one way to transmit electronic information over the telephone lines. They can transmit pictures and writing. If your computer has the appropriate software it can send a fax directly without printing the information first.

Fiber optic   Information of various kinds can be transferred over modern telephone fiber optic cables.

One fiber optic cable has enough room for information to carry all the telephone calls made in the United States at one time.

Footprint   Footprint is the area that a computer takes up on your desk.

Internal memory   Most software instructions are stored in the computer's internal memory until they are used.

Kilobyte (K's)   We measure how much information is stored on a chip by counting it in kilobytes, or K's. Each K is just over 1,000 bytes. 1 K = 1,024 bytes

Mainframe   Mainframe computers are large computers that are used by many people over a network.

Megabyte (MB)   1 megabyte (MB) is just over 1 million bytes. 1 MB = 1,024,000 bytes

Memory   Computers have three kinds of memory: Random Access Memory (RAM), Read Only Memory (ROM), and storage memory. Each of these kinds of memory has different purposes and characteristics. (See RAM, ROM, and memory storage.)

Memory chips   Memory chips are important because they can store or process very large amounts of information.

Memory storage	If we want to store or save information we can use hard disks (hard drives), floppy disks, or CD-ROM disks. If there is a great deal of information to store, tapes are often used.
Microprocessor	A microprocessor is a complete computer on a single chip.
Modems	Modems are electronic devices that allow computers to interact with each other over telephone lines. Modems have different speeds. The faster the modem the shorter the time it takes for information to get from one computer to another.
Operating system	The operating system contains the rules and techniques that control the way a computer works. Some computers can work with several operating systems.
Personal computers	The computers that most of us use are called personal computers, because they are used by one person at a time.
RAM	RAM is an abbreviation for Random Access Memory. RAM is the working part of the computer's memory. You can add and delete information from it. You can write, to add information to it. You can read, to find information and/or remove it. The information you place in RAM is there only when the computer is turned on. If you wish to save it you must use some form of memory-saving device.
ROM	ROM is short for Read Only Memory. ROM is built into the computer and can only be read. You cannot add or delete information from it. ROM contains the instructions and information that enable the computer to function.
Scanners	Scanners are electronic devices that allow us to turn photographs, drawings, or words directly into electronic data. We can then modify the input or use the data in documents.
Sensors	Sensors, which measure characteristics such as temperature, sound, and acidity, are used for inputting data directly into the computer.

Acknowledgments

Illustration

Kimble Mead: 1, 26-27, 60-61
Matt Straub: 2-5
Paragraphics: 6-7, 22-25, 55, 112
Elliot Kreloff: 8, 70-72, 105-106
Dave Joly: 9
Jim Paillot: 10-11, 56-57, 91-92, 130-131 133, 135, 137, 138, 141
David Brion: 12, 93
Dan Brawner: 13, 48
Patrick Merrell: 14-16, 52-53
Terry Sirrell: 17, 100-103
Debbie Tilley: 18-19, 73
Tim Haggerty: 20, 32-33, 63-67, 116-128
Stephen Schudlich: 21
Katherine Tillotson: 28-31, 95
Steve Henry: 34, 104
Jimminy Roux: 35
Daniel Del Valle: 36, charts–121, 122, 124, 126, 127, 128
Burton Morris: 37-41
Annie Gusman: 42
Kathy Saska: 43-45
Obadinah Heavner: 46
Luisa D'Augusta: 47, 69
Randy Verougstraete: 50, 84-85
Rachel Geswaldo: 51, 89
Alex Bloch: 54, 74-75, 94
Susan Swan: 62
Steve Sullivan: 68
Phil Marden: 76-77
Stephen Foster: 78
Jean Pidgeon: 79-80
Liisa Chauncy Guida: 81-82
Joe Boddy: 86-88
Claude Martinot: 96-97
Jennifer Hewitson: 98-99
Brad Gaber: 107-109
Marty Blake: 113-114
Jana Collins: 115
Karen Tully: border–116-128
Nikolai Punin: 129, 142-149

Photography

Photo Management: **Picture It Corporation**
Clara Aich: 22-25, 58, 60-61, 89, 124-125, 128
Kathryn Millan: 14-15, 59, 83, 122-125, 128
Photo Resource: **FPG Int.:** 115, 123

Technical Art

TCA Graphics Inc.: 8, 18, 20, 26, 39, 40, 41, 42, 44, 47, 49, 50, 58, 63, 69, 75, 79, 80, 83, 85, 90, 104, 110, 111, 116-120, 130-141